Guide to Adirondack Trails:

NORTHERN REGION

Second Edition
The Forest Preserve Series (2nd ed.), Volume II

By Peter V. O'Shea, Jr.
Series Editor, Neal Burdick

The Adirondack Mountain Club, Inc.

Copyright © 1986, 1994 by
The Adirondack Mountain Club, Inc.
All rights reserved.
Design by Idee Design, Glens Falls, NY
All page maps by Paul Fahey except the following,
    by Ted Koch: Pp. 37, 40, 48, 96, 127, 131, 134.

First Edition, 1986
Second Edition, 1994; rev. 1995, 1997

**Library of Congress Cataloging-in-
Publication Data**
O'Shea, Peter V.
    Guide to Adirondack Trails. Northern region / Peter V. O'Shea, Jr.
      —2nd ed.
        p. cm.—(The Forest preserve series. 2nd ed. ; v. 2)
    Includes index.
    ISBN 0-935272-63-1 : $16.95.—ISBN 0-935272-64-X (8-volume set)
    1. Hiking – New York (State)—Adirondack Park – Guidebooks.
2. Trails – New York (State)—Adirondack Park – Guidebooks.
3. Adirondack Park (N.Y.)—Guidebooks.   I. Adirondack Mountain Club. II. Title.
    III. Series.
GV199.42.N652A3457   1993   93-28566
796.5'1'097475—dc20   CIP

Printed in the
United States of America

We Welcome Your Letters!

ADK and its authors make every effort to keep our guidebooks up to date, however, trail conditions are always changing. If you note an error or discrepancy, or if you wish to forward a suggestion, we welcome your input. Please write us, Attn: Publications, citing book title, year of your edition, trail number, page number, and date of your observation. Thanks for your help.

Note: use of the information in this book is at the sole risk of the user.

Dedication

Clarence Petty
Roderick Fraser

Of all the noted woodsmen who have ranged the green forests and clear waterways of this section of the Adirondacks, perhaps none more clearly typifies the region than Clarence Petty.

Raised in the woods between Tupper Lake and Saranac Lake, Clarence has spent most of his life in them as a District Forest Ranger with the DEC. His love and appreciation of these woods have far transcended his employment; he has utilized every available opportunity to gain an intimate knowledge of the lore of the region. This knowledge he has readily and generously shared with others.

Upon retirement, Clarence became more active than ever as he took up the cause of the protection of his beloved Adirondacks. In this role he has courageously and effectively battled any and all threats to the Adirondack environment.

Just before this second edition went into production, Roderick Fraser of Star Lake, New York, a good friend and long-time woodsman, passed away. Rod had recently retired from the DEC as head of the St. Lawrence County trail crew, in which capacity he oversaw maintenance and construction of most of the trails described in this guide. Like Clarence Petty, he loved the woods and waterways of this northern region and left an indelible mark on them.

The wild brook trout in the remote headwater ponds will no longer be able to match their wits with a master angler. They, the forest itself and I will miss him.

This trail guide to the northern Adirondacks is gratefully dedicated to Clarence Petty and Rod Fraser.

PETER V. O'SHEA, JR.

Northern Region

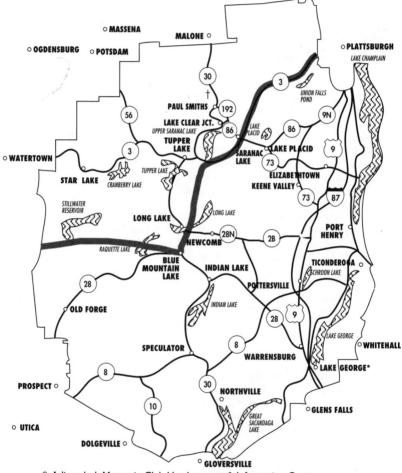

* Adirondack Mountain Club Headquarters & Information Center
† Visitor Interpretive Center

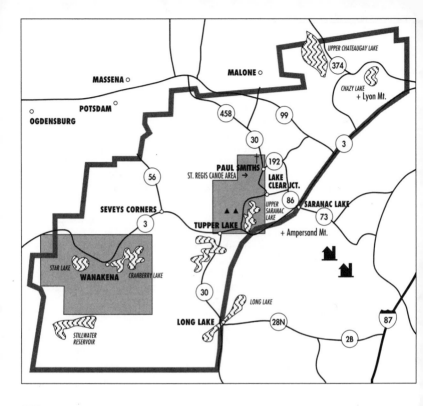

Northern region topo-map boundary

Northern region boundary line

Lakes

+ Mountains

† Visitor Interpretive Center

▲ Fish Creek & Rollins Pond campgrounds

 ADK s Adirondak Loj & High Peaks Information Center (left),
Johns Brook Lodge (right)

Attention!

Some of the effects of the awesome "microburst" storm of July 15, 1995, are still being experienced in parts of the area covered by this book as of April 1997. While all of the trails have been opened with the exception of those listed below, they remain in general rougher than before the storm due to upturned roots and trailside debris. Trees continue to fall even now, requiring the use of special caution in the woods, especially on windy days.

The following trails had still not been opened as of April 1997.

Trail No.	Name
59	Sand Lake Trail
60	Cage Lake Trail (from Sand Lake)
62	Cowhorn Junction Trail
64	Clear Pond Trail (from Cowhorn Jct.)
65	Deer Pond Trail (from Cowhorn Jct.)
66	Six Mile Creek Trail (from Cowhorn Jct.)
67	Cowhorn Pond Trail
76	Round Lake Trail
77	Round Lake Trail (from Kalurah)

Additional Changes

(58) High Falls Loop (via Leary Trail)

The Leary Trail segment of this popular loop has been abandoned due to the effects of the storm. High Falls is now reached by the High Falls truck trail—a distance of 9.2 mi. Continue straight ahead at the junction of the Leary Trail to reach High Falls. The rest of the Loop remains the same. The distances now are as follows: High Falls trailhead to High Falls, 9.2 mi.; to Sand Hill Jct., 12.2 mi.; to Janacks Landing, 13.1 mi.; to Dead Creek Flow, 14.2 mi.; to start of Dead Creek truck trail, 16.2 mi.; to point of beginning, 16.7 mi.

(73) Little River

The effects of the microburst have caused this trail to be abandoned. However, a recent state acquisition provides access to the Little River along a gated gravel road that remains open to reach a private inholding. The road ambles one mile; passing two entrancing kettle ponds lying on either side, to arrive at the river overlooking a 20-foot waterfall. The start of the trail is the gated road 0.4 mi. farther down Amo (also known as Lake) Rd.

Distances: Start of trail to Readway Ponds, 0.3 mi.; to jct. (go R), 0.9 mi.; to waterfall and river, 1.0 mi. As of April 1997 the camp belonging to the prior inholding still remained at the site here.

(75) Cage Lake Trail (via Boundary Trail)

This trail now terminates at Buck Pond for a total distance of 7.3 mi.

Additional Trail Closures

(47) Stone Dam Trail

A lack of signs and problems with the hunting club leases of adjoining corporate timberlands suggest this trail cannot be recommended. DEC is working to rectify this situation.

(71) Old Wanakena Road

This trail is impassable because of extensive beaver flooding along its midreaches.

The DEC hopes to re-open all of the trails that were closed as a direct result of the microburst. Trail crews began working in May of 1997. As trails are re-opened, announcement will be made in *Adirondac* magazine. Eventually all trails will be open (including changes listed) with the exception of nos. 47 and 71.

Preface

The northern region of the Adirondacks comprises the most secluded and isolated portion of the Adirondack Park. It is probably the least commercial area of the Adirondacks, an area where the old ways and manner of doing things have a tendency to linger after they have disappeared elsewhere. It is composed primarily of the entire area of the park in St. Lawrence County and most of that in Franklin County. The most extensive, rather isolated forests of this region are fondly known as the Great South Woods by residents of the St. Lawrence Valley who have been among its chief users over the years. It follows that most of the hiking trails in the region are at present little known to the general public at large.

The original edition of the Northern guide was an attempt to rectify that situation. This second edition is both an update and an enumeration of the numerous changes that have occurred in the intervening seven years since the first edition was published.

The changes have been profound indeed in this section of the Adirondack Park. Extensive acreage has been acquired both as additions to the Forest Preserve and as Conservation Easements; new trails have been constructed and a number of trails from the first edition have been officially abandoned by DEC and have been omitted from this second edition. Causes of abandonment vary: persistent beaver flooding, trailheads becoming inaccessible either physically or legally, remoteness of setting and consequent difficulty of maintenance, etc. The trails abandoned have been more than offset by the new trails and recently acquired acreage.

The extensive changes in this region have necessitated regrouping the area trails into 12 general sections instead of the original five.

With the reorganization of chapters, a number of trails in the first edition have been placed in different sections. These sections are defined by various parameters: central hamlets, Forest Preserve classifications and land tracts or geologic features. In addition, various outlying trails have been added to each appropriate section in the interest of cohesion. Each chapter is introduced by a short section briefly outlining and describing the area and furnishing a synopsis of the trails included therein.

All trails in this generally level to rolling region can be assumed to be moderate in grade unless stated specifically to the contrary. Generally, these exceptions occur only on the relatively few ascents to the summits of the region's outlying peaks. Distances are usually one-way; round trip distances will be double the total given.

Many trail junction to trail junction segments have been given as complete trails rather than as legs of longer trails to more popular destinations. The hiker may, by referring to the text and the guide maps enclosed, determine which of the destinations accessible from a junction he or she may wish to proceed to and in what order. Several short trails connecting longer routes have also been described separately; their main function, however, is to extend these longer routes into convenient circuits. The extensive system of trails in several of the sections lends itself admirably to a chain of lengthy circuits and occasionally modified loops; the most noteworthy of these are included at the ends of the appropriate chapters.

The trails in general proceed through an attractive maturing forest of mixed hardwoods and conifers. They pass extensive areas of some of the most haunting boreal wetlands in the entire Northeast on their way to connecting many of the myriad ponds and lakes that lie strewn like pearls in a random-shaped necklace throughout the region. The region's isolation has assured that the trails have remained relatively uncluttered. Indeed, a few of the more remote trails in the region are only sporadically marked and may be indistinct paths, especially in their middle reaches.

Caution should be exercised in these cases, noted in the text. Many of the trails were marked originally as snowmobile trails; they have been included where suitable for hiking. This is invariably the case, except where excess wetness prevails. Another feature of the trails in this region is the amount of beaver flooding they are subjected to. If passage cannot be made on the dam itself, a bushwhack around the flooded area will be necessary in order to regain the trail.

Many of the trails in this region were originally laid out as logging railroads at or before the turn of the century, and subsequently converted to truck trails by the CCC during the Depression years. Vehicular traffic is now prohibited on them, making them excellent as hiking trails. They are included here in their entirety as complete trails when they go through ecologically important or aesthetically pleasing areas. Otherwise, ancillary trails which branch off and then return, thereby shortening the total distance to their destination, are utilized in the interest of brevity. One example of the latter is the Hayes Brook Truck Trail which continues through a monotonous pine plantation after the marked ski trail leaves it.

The many truck trails provide excellent conduits for cross-country skiing in the region. The abundant snowfall and rolling terrain of the area add to the skier's pleasure. All the area trails have been analyzed for their suitability as cross-country ski routes; their appropriateness as such is indicated in their specific description.

A number of the larger lakes of the region have DEC campsites on their shores. Included here are Cranberry Lake, Forked Lake, Lake Eaton, Meacham Lake, Buck Pond (near Onchiota in the far eastern part of the region), Fish Creek Ponds, and Rollins Pond. All, especially the latter two, receive heavy usage during the summer months. They are the starting point for several of the trails described in this guide and also provide a convenient camping site for exploring trails in the general vicinity. Their locations are described in Appendix V.

Since the inception of the DEC's Park Ranger Program in 1978, much information has been obtained on how to prevent the continued physical deterioration of heavily used backcountry areas. This has resulted in the promulgation and enforcement of some new regulations concerning camping. Early indications are that these regulations have successfully halted much of the deterioration, making unnecessary a cumbersome and restrictive permit system to reduce overall use. Thus each hiker has the responsibility to obey these regulations, not only out of fear of the legal consequences, but also because compliance will prevent deterioration of these beautiful wilderness lands and therefore enhance the experience of all who follow.

Finally, I would like to offer my warmest gratitude to all those many individuals whose generous assistance made the completion of this trail guide a reality. Among those who spring specifically to mind are DEC foresters John Kramer and James Papero, whose excellent unit management plans and trail knowledge in their respective areas proved invaluable to me along the way. Also invaluable was the assistance rendered by DEC forest ranger Terry Perkins. He truly typifies the ideal of the forest ranger force. Special thanks also to the Publications Committee of the Adirondack Mountain Club, whose commitment to the ADK Forest Preserve Series has made this project possible, and to my good friend and fellow Laurentian Chapter member Mimi Moulton of Potsdam, New York, who cheerfully typed page after page of handwritten manuscript for this guide. Without her aid this second edition of the guide would not exist.

Peter V. O'Shea, Jr.
Fine, New York
April 1993

Contents

Page Maps

Betsy Tisdale

Lampson Falls

Introduction

The Adirondack Mountain Club Forest Preserve Series

The Forest Preserve Series of Guides to Adirondack and Catskill Trails covers all hiking opportunities on the approximately 2.75 million acres of public Forest Preserve land in the Adirondack and Catskill parks. The Adirondack Mountain Club (ADK) published the first guidebook in this series over sixty years ago with the idea that hiking guides would eventually cover all Forest Preserve lands; it is appropriate that the completion of this series coincided with the decade-long centennial celebration of the enactment of the Forest Preserve legislation. Each guide in this series, listed below, has been revised within the last few years.

Vol. I: *Guide to Adirondack Trails: High Peaks Region*
Vol. II: *Guide to Adirondack Trails: Northern Region*
Vol. III: *Guide to Adirondack Trails: Central Region*
Vol. IV: *Guide to Adirondack Trails: Northville-Placid Trail*
Vol. V: *Guide to Adirondack Trails: West-Central Region*
Vol. VI: *Guide to Adirondack Trails: Eastern Region*
Vol. VII: *Guide to Adirondack Trails: Southern Region*
Vol. VIII: Guide to Catskill Trails

The public lands that constitute the Adirondack Forest Preserve are unique among all other wild public lands in the United States because they enjoy constitutional protection against sale or development. The story of this unique protection begins with the earliest history of the Adirondacks as recounted below, and it continues today as groups such as the Adirondack Mountain Club strive to guard this constitutional protection. The protection of many of the scenic and aesthetic resources of the Forest Preserve also rests with the individual hiker who has the responsibility not to degrade these resources in any way while enjoying their wonders. The Forest Preserve Series of trail guides seeks not only to show hikers where to hike but also to interpret the area's natural and social history and offer guidelines whereby users can minimize their impact on the land.

The Adirondacks

The Adirondack region of northern New York is unique in many ways. It contains the only mountains in the eastern U.S. that are not geologically Appalachian. In the late 1800s it was the first forested area in the nation to benefit from enlightened conservation measures. At roughly the same time it was also the most prestigious resort area in the country. In the twentieth century, the Adirondacks became the only place in the Western Hemisphere to host two winter Olympiads. In the 1970s the region was the first of significant size in the nation to experience comprehensive land use controls. The Adirondack Forest Preserve (see below) is part of the only wild lands preserve in the nation whose fate lies in the hands of the voters of the entire state in which it is located.

Geologically, the Adirondacks are part of the Canadian Shield, a vast terrane of ancient Precambrian igneous and metamorphic rock that underlies about half of Canada and constitutes the nucleus of the North American continent. In the U.S. the Shield bedrock mostly lies concealed under younger Paleozoic sedimentary rock strata, but it is well exposed in a few regions, among them the Adirondacks. The Adirondacks are visibly connected across the Thousand Islands to the Grenville Province of the eastern side of the Shield, which is around one billion years old.

Upward doming of the Adirondack mass in the past few million years – a process that is still going on – is responsible for the erosional stripping of the younger rock cover and exposure of the ancient bedrock. The rocks here are mainly gneisses of a wide range of composition. One of the more interesting and geologically puzzling rocks is the enormous anorthosite mass that makes up nearly all of the High Peaks region. A nearly monomineralic rock composed of plagioclase feldspar, this particular rock was apparently formed at depths of up to fifteen miles below the surface. It is nearly identical to some of the rock brought back from the moon.

The present Adirondack landscape is geologically young, a product of erosion initiated by the ongoing doming. The stream-carved topography has been extensively modified by the sculpturing of glaciers which, on at least four widely separated occasions during the Ice Age, completely covered the mountains.

Ecologically, the Adirondacks are part of a vegetation transition zone, with the northern, largely coniferous boreal forest (from the Greek god Boreas, owner of the north wind, whose name can be found on a mountain peak and series of ponds in the High Peaks region) and the southern deciduous forest, exemplified by beech/maple stands, intermingling to present a pleasing array of forest tree species. Different vegetation zones are also encountered as one ascends the higher mountains in the Adirondacks; the tops of the highest peaks are truly arctic, with mosses and lichens that are common hundreds of miles to the north.

A rugged and heavily forested region, the Adirondacks were generally not hospitable to native Americans, who used the region principally for hunting and occasionally for fighting. Remnants of ancient campgrounds have been found in some locations. The native legacy survives principally in such place names as Indian Carry, on the Raquette River-Saranac Lakes canoe route, and the Oswegatchie River in the northwest Adirondacks.

The first white man to see the Adirondacks was likely the French explorer Jacques Cartier, who on his first trip up the St. Lawrence River in 1535 stood on top of Mont Royal (now within the city of Montreal) and discerned high ground to the south. Closer looks were had by Samuel de Champlain and Henry Hudson, who came from the north and south, respectively, by coincidence within a few weeks of each other in 1609.

For the next two centuries the Champlain Valley to the east of the Adirondacks was a battleground. Iroquois, Algonquin, French, British and eventually American fighters struggled for control over the valley and with it supremacy over the continent. Settlers slowly filled the St. Lawrence Valley to the north, the Mohawk Valley to the south, and somewhat later the Black River Valley to the west. Meanwhile the vast, rolling forests of the interior slumbered in virtual anonymity, disturbed only by an occasional hunter, timber cruiser or wanderer.

With the coming of the 19th century, people discovered the Adirondacks. Virtually unknown as late as the 1830s (the source of the Nile River was located before the source of the Hudson), by 1850 the Adirondacks made New York the leading timber producing state in the nation. This distinction did not last for long, though, as the supply of timber was quickly brought close to extinction. Meanwhile, mineral resources, particularly iron, were being exploited.

After the Civil War, people began to look toward the Adirondacks for recreation as well as for financial gain. An economic boom, increasing acceptability of leisure time, and the publication of a single book, *Adventures in the Wilderness* by the Rev. William H. H. Murray in 1869, combined to create a veritable flood of vacationers descending upon the Adirondacks. To serve them, a new industry, characterized by grand hotels and rustic guides, sprang up. Simultaneously, thanks to the pioneering work of Dr. Edward Livingston Trudeau, the Adirondacks, particularly the

Saranac Lake area, became known far and wide as a mecca for tubercular patients.

In the decades following the Civil War the idea of conservation began to take on some legitimacy, thanks in large part to the book *Man and Nature* written by George Perkins Marsh in 1864. In this remarkably influential book, which noted historian Lewis Mumford once called "the fountainhead of the American conservation movement," Marsh called for the implementation of such practices as reforestation and watershed protection, and suggested that the Adirondacks were a good laboratory for testing these ideas.

Another trend in the middle decades of the 19th century was an increasing acceptance of wilderness. This was brought about partly through the work of poets such as William Cullen Bryant, writers such as Henry David Thoreau, and artists such as Frederick Church. Also contributing to this trend was the fact that, as the frontier moved steadily westward, the wilderness was no longer seen as a physical threat, at least not in the more populous, affluent East.

Vacationers, tubercular patients, conservationists, wilderness devotees – all of these people wanted to see the resources of the Adirondacks preserved. This was partially achieved in 1885, when, after much political wrangling, the New York State legislature created the Adirondack Forest Preserve and directed that "the lands now or hereafter constituting the Forest Preserve shall be forever kept as wild forest lands." This action marked the first time a state government had set aside a significant piece of wilderness for reasons other than its scenic uniqueness.

In 1892, the legislature created the Adirondack State Park, consisting of Adirondack Forest Preserve land plus all privately owned land within a somewhat arbitrary boundary surrounding the Adirondacks, known as the "blue line" because it was drawn in blue on a large state map when it was first established. In 1894, in response to continuing abuses of the Forest Preserve law, the state's voters approved the inclusion of the "forever wild" portion of that law in the constitution of New York State, thus creating the only preserve in the nation that has constitutional protection. Today the Forest Preserve consists of 2.5 million acres, being those lands owned by the people of the State of New York that are within the 6-million-acre Adirondack State Park, which is the largest park in the nation outside of Alaska.

In the first decade of the 20th century, raging fires consumed hundreds of thousands of acres of prime Adirondack forest lands; the scars from these fires can still be seen in many locations, both in exposed rock and in vegetation patterns. After World War I, tourism gradually took over as the primary industry in the Adirondacks. The arrival of the automobile, the invention of theme parks (some of the very first of which were in the Adirondacks), the development of winter sports facilities (with Lake Placid hosting the Winter Olympics in 1932), the increasing popularity of camping and hiking, and the growth of the second-home industry all brought such pressures to bear on the region that in 1968 Governor Nelson Rockefeller created a Temporary Study Commission on the Future of the Adirondacks. This commission made 181 recommendations, chief among them that a comprehensive land use plan, covering both public and private lands, be put in place and administered. This was accomplished by 1973, with the creation of the land use plans and the Adirondack Park Agency to manage them. While the plans and the Agency have remained controversial, they are indicative of the need to address the issues facing the Adirondacks boldly and innovatively.

In 1990, there were 130,000 permanent residents and 100,000 seasonal residents in the 9375-square-mile Adirondack Park, which is roughly the size of Vermont. Recreation, forestry, mining and agriculture are the principal industries in the park.

The Northern Region

The trails described in this book are all in the northern part of Adirondack Park. These trails are mainly in the St. Lawrence and Franklin County portions of the Adirondacks in the northwestern and north-central parts of the Park. The area includes the villages of Star Lake, Cranberry Lake, Tupper Lake and Paul Smiths. The principal highways in the region are NY 3 and NY 30, with NY 3 forming the southern boundary of the region in the north-central section and Stillwater Reservoir and the abandoned Remsen-to-Lake Placid railroad tracks generally forming the southern boundary in the northwestern section. The northern boundary of the region corresponds to the northern boundary of the Adirondack Park.

Using This Guidebook

Like all the books in the Adirondack Mountain Club Forest Preserve Series of Guides to Adirondack Trails, this book is intended to be both a reference tool for planning trips and a field guide to carry on the trail. All introductory material should be read carefully, for it contains important information regarding the use of this book, as well as numerous suggestions for safe and proper travel by foot in the Adirondacks. For campers, there is an important section on the relevant rules and regulations for camping in the Adirondacks.

The introductions to each of the sections in this book will give hikers an idea of the varied opportunities available in the northern region. There are many beautiful and seldom-visited places aside from the popular hiking, climbing and camping areas; this guide will enable you to find and explore these remote spots.

Almost every trail in this book is suitable for snowshoeing;

crampons are recommended for the few mountain ascents. Skiing suitability is discussed in the "Trail in Winter" section of each trail description.

Maps

The map enclosed in the back of this book is a composite of U.S. Geological Survey quadrangles with updated overlays of trails, shelters and private land lines. This map is especially valuable because of its combination of contour lines from the original base maps and recent trail information, updated with each printing of this guide. The map covers much of the terrain described in this guide-book, but a number of trails not conveniently shown on it are shown on individual page maps within the text. Extra copies of the two-sided Northern Region map are available from many retailers or directly from the Adirondack Mountain Club, 814 Goggins Rd., Lake George, NY 12845-4117.

There are now three series of USGS maps covering this area. One series is the familiar 15-minute series which was produced mainly in the mid-1950s. Another is the 7.5-minute series which was issued mostly in the 1960s. A recent addition to these two has been the issuance of a new 7.5 by 15-minute series with metric elevation and contours. The USGS produced this series late in the 1970s in anticipation of the 1980 Winter Olympics, and the metric units reflect the international flavor of the event. Only the 7.5-minute series of the 1960s shows Forest Preserve land; however, much acreage has been added to the preserve since this series was pro-duced. The map included with this guidebook uses all of these series of maps.

Trail Signs and Markers

With normal alertness to one's surroundings, trails in the Adirondacks are easy to follow. In most cases, where trails leave a highway or come to a junction there will be a sign to direct the hiker. As much as possible, descriptions in this guidebook are detailed enough so that a hiker can find the correct route even in the rare cases when signs are temporarily down. The trails themselves are usually marked with metal disks bearing the insignia of the organization responsible for them. Trails maintained by the DEC are marked with blue, yellow or red disks; the particular color for each trail is indicated on the signs and in the guidebook description.

In addition to a map, all hikers should carry a compass and know at least the basics of its use. In some descriptions, this guide uses compass bearings to differentiate the trail at a junction or to indicate the direction of travel above timberline. More importantly, a compass can be an indispensable aid in the event that you lose your way.

The trails in the northern region, however, differ in a number of respects from the trails present in the rest of the Adirondacks. Many of the trails described here were originally laid out as snowmobile trails and are marked as such by the DEC with large, light orange disks. On some of these trails the markers now appear only sporadically. (There are other trails that are currently unmarked either partially or in their entirety; these usually pass through fairly recent additions to the Forest Preserve. These have been included when they can be followed without too much difficulty.) To complete the assortment of different trail types there are a number of trails included that are marked as horse trails or as canoe carries. In general, the small yellow disks of the canoe carries are clearly indicated, while the horse trail disks have not been kept up as well. There is one trail over private property included – the red-marked nature trail through the forest lands of Paul Smiths College.

All other trails described in this guide are on public land or along public rights of way but there may be "posted" signs at some points. These are usually there to remind hikers that they are on private land over which the owner has kindly granted permission for hikers to pass. In most cases, leaving the trail, camping, fishing and hunting are not permitted on these lands, and hikers should respect the owner's wishes.

Distance and Time

All distances along the trails in this guidebook have been measured by means of a pedometer. This makes possible generally accurate readings to a tenth of a mile. Pedometer accuracy has been double-checked both against the stride of an individual and against the odometer of a motor vehicle. Rechecking for accuracy was done on a regular basis, using different vehicles.

At the start of each section of this guide there is a list of trails in the region, the mileage unique to the trail, and the number of the page on which the trail description is located. All mileage distances given are cumulative, the beginning of the trail being the 0 mi. point. A distance summary is given at the end of each trail description with the total distance expressed in kilometers as well as in miles. To the inexperienced hiker, these distances will seem longer on the trail, but he or she will quickly learn that there is a great difference between "sidewalk" miles and "trail" miles.

The distances given in this guide are often at odds with the distances given on the DEC trail signs. The DEC has used a variety of measuring methods over the years and has not always updated every sign after every change of distance caused by rerouting, etc. In all cases where there is a disagreement, the guidebook distance can be assumed to be correct.

No attempt has been made to estimate times for these trails. A conservative rule to follow in estimating time is to allow an hour for every 1.5 mi., plus ½ hour for each 1000 ft. ascended with experience soon indicating how close each hiker is to this standard. Most day hikers will probably hike faster than this, but backpackers will probably find they go more slowly.

Abbreviations and Conventions

In each of the books in the Forest Preserve Series, R and L, with periods omitted, are used for right and left. The R and L banks of a stream are determined by looking downstream. Likewise, the R fork of a stream is on the R when one faces downstream. N, S, E and W, again without periods, are used for north, south, east and west. Some compass directions are given in degrees, figuring from true N, with E as 90 degrees, etc.

The following abbreviations are used in the text and on the maps:

ADK	Adirondack Mountain Club
APA	Adirondack Park Agency
CCC	Civilian Conservation Corps (Depression era)
DEC	New York State Department of Environmental Conservation
USGS	United States Geological Survey
YCC	Youth Conservation Corps (St. Lawrence County)
4WD	Four-wheel-drive vehicle
ft.	feet
km	kilometer or kilometers
m	meter or meters
mi.	mile or miles
yds.	yards

Hiking with Children

Most hikers with children want to start them hiking as early as possible, but one needs to be aware that children can have very different perceptions of what it means to go on a hike. Given the range of physical abilities and mental outlooks, there is no one "right" way to introduce a child to the concept of struggling up a steep hill only to turn around and return to the starting point. The guidelines below may help avoid a few of the common pitfalls. Also, see Appendix III for a table of short hikes in the region.

Attitude:

Having a positive experience is more important than reaching one's destination. At least at first, children are not goal-oriented, so that the promise of reaching the view at the top does not have the same motivation factor it has for adults. Be prepared to stop short of the original goal; as one experienced father put it, "You are where you are." Make an adventure out of the tough spots ("we're almost to the 'mountain goat pitch' ") and a game out of boring spots ("how many trail markers can you see?"). Be prepared to stop and look at anything of interest, whether it is you or the child who notices the plant, frog, moss, stick, leaf or whatever. A lady-slipper along the trail may be an adult's greatest treat, but a child will take even greater pleasure in finding a stick that looks vaguely like a dinosaur.

Make sure to reward the child for completing a hike. Make it a special occasion, perhaps a reason for a call to the grandparents or a favorite desert with dinner. You may want to keep a chart or map of hikes done to show progress. Show the child the day's trip on a map, and get it out again to plan the next one. Over time, most children will come to appreciate the satisfaction of a fun hike, and will want to do more.

Distance and Destination:

Three-year-olds (and even strong two-year-olds) can hike as much as a mile, and a mile will get you to the top of some small mountains. Walking uphill can be a problem, however, and many children are just as excited to hike a flat route to a stream where they can throw rocks and sticks. Four- to six-year-olds are more likely to be able to focus on making an ascent of over a mile to a summit – but again, too much steep going can prove discouraging.

Time:

At least double your own time for a particular hike. Children not only walk more slowly but also want to take frequent breaks. Have an open-ended time schedule so that you don't become impatient with slower-than-expected progress. Adult hikers know that a steady pace with fewer stops is usually the most efficient, but children need to take "mental" breaks as well as physical rests. While actually hiking, however, encourage steady progress as opposed to the "20 running steps followed by a complete stop" type of pace that many children will try at first.

Equipment and Supplies:

Even small children should be encouraged to carry at least some of their own gear, but be prepared to take it if the pack seems to be the only thing causing an unpleasant time. Bring plenty of water and food and don't feel that your goal is to instill toughness by forcing the march to the summit before the first sip of water can be had. On a hot day, freeze a few plastic water bottles beforehand. Not only will you have cool water, but watching the ice melt and telling others about a "special hiking trick" will add to the hike in ways an adult could never understand. Likewise, avoid using food (i.e. candy) as a bribe too often, but I doubt if there are many parents who can claim never to have promised a treat for just a little more effort. Bring insect repellent; a cap can be very helpful in keeping the bugs off the back of the head.

Hiking boots are the preferred footwear, but running shoes are fine as long as they are sturdy enough to offer protection from sharp rocks underneath and sticks above. Make sure the child wears socks and has a sweater and raincoat at all times. Add a wool hat and mittens if it is at all cold because a summit can be much colder. Long pants offer protection from twigs and brambles as well as reducing the exposed skin area for insect bites, but don't push it if the child prefers shorts.

Most importantly, double-check that every needed item is indeed packed. One forgotten cookie can ruin the whole trip.

Safety:

Children have very little judgment and, at first, virtually no ability to stay on even an "obvious" trail. Let them lead but keep them in sight, and be ready to take the lead near any cliffs, bridges or other dangerous areas. Be especially careful on top of ledges and keep them from throwing anything over the edge of a cliff. Not only is it very easy for a child to throw himself off as well, but there may be others below. Children love to hike with the family dog, but large, rambunctious dogs pose the danger of knocking a child down or even off the trail as they race back and forth checking on everyone or chasing sticks.

Above all, keep the group together and never solve the problem of a reluctant hiker by sending him back down the trail alone. The above list of safety concerns is hardly complete, but it may alert parents to a few of the potential problems unique to hiking.

Wilderness Camping

It is not the purpose of this series to teach one how to camp in the woods. There are many good books available on that subject, which are more comprehensive and useful than any explanation that could be given in the space available here. The information below should, however, serve to make hikers aware of the differences and peculiarities of the Adirondacks while giving strong emphasis to currently recommended procedures to reduce environmental damage – particularly in heavily used areas.

Except for Johns Brook Lodge, 3.5 mi. up the Marcy trail (the Phelps Trail) from Keene Valley, there are no huts in the Adirondacks. There are, however, lean-tos at many convenient locations along the trails, and there are also many possibilities for tenting along the way. The regulations regarding tenting and the use of these shelters are simple and unrestricted when compared to those of other popular backpacking areas in the country; but it is important that every backpacker know and obey the restrictions that do exist, since they are designed to promote the long-term enjoyment of the greatest number of people.

General Camping Guidelines:

Except for groups of ten or more and smaller groups who wish to camp at one location for more than three nights (see below), no camping or fire permits are required in the Adirondacks, but campers must obey all DEC regulations regarding camping. Listed below are some of the most important regulations. Complete regulations are available from the DEC and are posted at most access points.

1) No camping within 150 ft. of a stream, other water source, or trail except at a designated campsite. Most areas near an existing lean-to are considered designated campsites; other areas are designated with the following symbol:

2) Except in an emergency, no camping is permitted above 4000 ft. in elevation. (This rule does not apply from December 1 to April 30.)

3) All washing of dishes must be done at least 150 ft. from any stream, pond, or other water source. **No soap**, even so-called "biodegradeable" soap, should ever get into the water, so use a pot to carry water at least 150 ft. away from your source and wash items and dispose of water there. One can also take a surprisingly effective bath by taking a quick dip and then using a pot for soaping and rinsing away from the stream or pond.

4) All human excrement must be buried under at least four inches of dirt at a spot at least 150 ft. away from any water source, and all toilet paper likewise buried or burned. Use established privies or latrines when available.

5) No wood except for **dead** and **down** timber may be used for fire building. Good wood is often scarce at popular campsites, so a stove is highly recommended.

6) No fire should be built near or on any flammable material. Much of the forest cover in the Adirondacks is composed of recently rotted twigs, leaves, or needles and is **highly flammable**. Build a fire at an established fireplace or on rocks or sand. Before leaving, destroy all traces of any new fireplace created.

7) All refuse must be completely burned or carried out of the woods. **Do not bury** any refuse and be sure that no packaging to be burned contains metal foil – it will not burn no matter how hot the

fire. Remember – if you carried it in, you can carry it out.

8) In general, leave no trace of your presence when leaving a campsite, and help out by carrying out *more* than you carried in.

Lean-tos:

Lean-tos are available on a first-come, first-served basis up to the capacity of the shelter – usually about seven persons. A small party cannot therefore claim exclusive use of a shelter and *must* allow late arrivals equal use. Most lean-tos have a fireplace in front (sometimes with a primitive grill) and sanitary facilities. Most are located near some source of water, but each camper must use his own judgment as to whether or not the water supply needs purification before drinking.

It is in very poor taste to carve or write one's initials in a shelter. Please try to keep these rustic shelters in good condition and appearance.

Since reservations cannot be made for any of these shelters, it is best to carry a tent or other alternate shelter. Many shelters away from the standard routes, however, are rarely used, and a small party can often find a shelter open in the more remote areas.

The following regulations apply specifically to lean-tos, in addition to the general camping regulations listed above:

1) No plastic may be used to close off the front of a shelter.

2) No nails or other permanent fastener may be used to affix a tarp in a lean-to, but it is permissible to use rope to tie canvas or nylon tarps across the front.

3) No tent may be pitched inside a lean-to,

Groups:

Any group of ten or more persons or smaller groups intending to camp at one location three nights or longer must obtain a permit *before* camping on state land. This system is designed to prevent overuse of certain critical sites and also to encourage groups to split into smaller parties more in keeping with the natural environment. Permits can be obtained from the DEC forest ranger closest to the actual starting point of one's proposed trip. The local forest ranger can be contacted by writing to him directly; if in doubt about whom to write, send the letter to the Department of Environmental Conservation, Ray Brook, NY 12977. They will forward the letter, but allow at least a week for the letter to reach the appropriate forest ranger.

One can also make the initial contact with the forest ranger by phone, but keep in mind that rangers' schedules during the busy summer season are often unpredictable. Forest rangers are listed in the white pages of local phone books under "New York, State of; Environmental Conservation, Department of; Forest Ranger." Bear in mind when calling that most rangers operate out of their private homes, and observe the normal courtesy used when calling a private residence. Contact by letter is much preferred, and, as one can see, camping with a large group requires careful planning several weeks before the trip.

Drinking Water

For many years, hikers could trust practically any water source in the Adirondacks to be pure and safe to drink. Unfortunately, as in many other mountain areas, some Adirondack water sources have become contaminated with a parasite known as *Giardia lamblia.* This intestinal parasite causes a disease known as Giardiasis – often called "Beaver Fever." It can be spread by any warm-blooded mammal when infected feces wash into the water; beavers are prime agents in transferring this parasite because they spend so much of their time near water. Hikers themselves have also become primary agents in spreading this disease since some individuals appear to be unaffected carriers of the disease, and other recently infected individuals may inadvertently spread the parasite before their symptoms become apparent.

Prevention: Follow the guidelines for the disposal of human excrement as stated in the section "Wilderness Camping" (above). Equally important, make sure that every member of your group is aware of the problem and follows the guidelines as well. The health of a fellow hiker may depend on your consideration.

Choosing a Water Source: While no water source can be guaranteed to be safe, smaller streams high in the mountains which have no possibility of a beaver dam or temporary human presence upstream are usually safe to drink. If, however, there is any doubt, treat the water before drinking.

Treatment: Boil all water for 2-3 minutes, administer an iodine-based chemical purifier (available at camping supply stores and some drug and department stores), or use a commercial filter designed specifically for Giardiasis prevention. If after returning from a trip you experience recurrent intestinal problems, consult your physician and explain your potential problem.

Wildlife

One of the most distinctive aspects of the northern region lies in the uniqueness of its fauna. This uniqueness applies from the perspective of both quality and quantity, for the region not only possesses some common species in optimum numbers for the Adirondacks as a whole but also harbors certain wildlife species that are considered rare, endangered or even officially extirpated in New York State. This faunal distinctiveness results from a blend of reasons both social and natural in origin.

The primary social factor in accounting for the wildlife quality lies in the relatively late settlement of the region by the descendants of European man. This has resulted in the prevailing mixture of large blocks of private land interspersed with Forest Preserve lands that characterizes the region today. The extensive private woodlands are now subject to lumbering while the Forest Preserve lands are constitutionally protected from cutting. The resulting mix of mature and cut-over woodlands provides the ideal ingredients for wildlife survival in a climate with winters as severe as those in the Adirondacks. The lumbered lands furnish plentiful browse and cover for hares, voles, and other small prey species while at the same time providing this browse in proximity to the uncut conifer stands of the Forest Preserve. The latter form the ideal composition of a winter deer yard. Since winter mortality is the main limiting factor for deer in the Adirondacks, it comes as no surprise that the northern region has the highest population of this large herbivore prey species in the entire Adirondacks. The abundance of these various prey species leads to a consequent high population of predators in the region.

The natural reasons for the region's wildlife uniqueness are twofold. The first is the occurrence of remote, mature stands of timber in the Forest Preserve. The second is the presence of extensive tracts of boreal forests throughout the region. These conifer stands are found covering both the excessively wet soils of the region's numerous bogs and swamps, and the excessively dry soils of the many eskers and other types of glacial outwash in the region. These vast boreal forests and secluded wilderness tracts have led to both the survival of certain rare northern fauna and the recolonization by other wilderness-associated species that were formerly extirpated. Some notable examples of the latter include moose (albeit sparingly at this time) and Canada lynx (sporadic). In addition to these two, the region has probably had more of the currently unverified reports of cougars than the other regions of the Adirondacks.

The status of some species typical of the Adirondack wilderness in this Forest Preserve centennial year of 1985 is as follows:

Black bear: Abundant in the region; special precautions should be taken with foodstuffs around campsites at night.

Eastern coyote: Has increased dramatically since its appearance during the 1930s. The animal, possibly of hybrid origin, has probably contributed to decreasing bobcat population in the area through direct competition.

Bobcat: Occurs in low to moderate numbers throughout the region. The bobcat was more abundant until the population explosion of the Eastern coyote beginning in the 1950s. Recent studies do show, however, that the bobcat requires a more extensive home range in the Adirondacks than in the Catskills.

Fisher: Abundant; fisher numbers come close to reaching maximum levels in the Adirondacks and in this region in particular.

Porcupine: Numbers controlled mainly by size of fisher population. When fisher populations are low (mostly due to a succession of open, competitive trapping seasons), porcupines undergo a population explosion.

Marten: Have recently extended their range into the region from their stronghold in the High Peaks.

Moose: Have also recently re-occupied former habitat in the region, arriving here mostly via northern Vermont with possibly some coming from Canada. The ratio of bull moose to cow moose in the Adirondacks is out of proportion due to the greater tendency of males to wander out of their home ranges in Canada and New England.

Canada lynx: Also appear to have a small population in the area, perhaps only a fluctuating one. Records of DEC show that two have been killed in the region in the past 20 years while a third was taken just outside the area. The recent re-introduction undertaken by SUNY College of Environmental Science and Forestry should ultimately result in a more stable lynx population in the Adirondack Park.

Cougar: As with moose, the reports of cougar sightings in the Adirondacks seem to be concentrated in this region. These increased sightings have been accompanied by plaster casts being made of tracks by qualified individuals in a number of instances. Most observers deem it fitting that a number of this allegedly extirpated species returned to the Forest Preserve in the centennial year of 1985.

The preceding species, typical of wilderness or semi-wilderness areas, are not likely to be encountered by the average Forest Preserve hiker. Exceptions would be the ubiquitous black bear arriving for a handout at a campsite at night, and the Eastern coyote howling near the campsite at dusk. There are, however, certain species which will be very much in evidence to an observant hiker:

Beaver: Its presence is seen everywhere in flooded trails, etc. Beaver may also be seen frequently swimming in rivers and lakes in the region towards dusk as they go out to repair dams and gather food.

Otter: Can occasionally be seen, particularly by canoeists, even during the daytime. During daylight hours they occasionally sun themselves on large boulders in a river or on the shore of a remote lake.

Red squirrel and **eastern chipmunk:** Are the two most abundantly seen mammals; they are seemingly everywhere and in almost all habitats in the region.

Hare: Will be noticed towards dusk along the sides of the trail.

Deer mouse, woodland jumping mouse, and porcupines: Will all be encountered at one time or another near the campsite at night. The handsome roan-colored woodland jumping mouse will be especially likely to be encountered near a campsite on the banks of a river or stream.

If it is true that the quality of wildlife is the hallmark of excellence in a region, as has often been stated, then it is indeed also true that the northern region of the Adirondacks is an area well endowed with the qualities of excellence.

Safety in the Northern Region

Although possessing only a minimum of exposed summits (none truly alpine) and steep terrain, the northern region does have abundant climatic hazards of its own. These center around the heavy snows and extremely low temperatures generally present from November until April. The region receives the tail-end of the lake-effect snowstorms blowing off Lake Ontario in the winter, thereby insuring usually deep snow even in the lowlands. Temperatures can dip to -40° F in winter; record lows well below this have been recorded at Stillwater Reservoir, Wanakena, and the village of Owls Head in Franklin County. It follows that caution should be exercised while hiking this region in winter. It is imperative that persons travel in groups of not less than four and be outfitted properly when winter conditions prevail. For more information on winter travel, see the ADK publication *Winterwise* by John Dunn.

This deep snow and extreme cold does have the effect, however, of preventing the colonization of the northern region by a number of noxious pests that are well known to the hiking fraternity in the more temperate parts of New York State. These include poison ivy, ticks, and both of the poisonous snakes occurring in the state: the timber rattlesnake and the copperhead.

As noted above, bears are abundant and pose a potential threat to personal safety unless due care is taken around the campsite at night. This should include securing food out of reach at all times, and never attempting to annoy or aggravate bears under any circumstances. Further information on this subject can be obtained in a pamphlet on bears issued by the ADK entitled "Bear Facts."

Another potential threat to hiker safety in this region occurs in the remoteness of a few of the trails and their consequent sporadic marking and indistinctness in certain spots. This subject is covered at more length in the Preface.

Finally, it must be said that the abundance of wetlands that enhances the wildlife dimension here probably also gives rise to a more abundant population of noxious insects. In addition, the shortage of wind-swept upper slopes inevitably gives hikers less relief from the attention of these biting flies and mosquitoes. A good insect repellent, preferably one containing the ingredient DEET, and long-sleeved shirt are recommended when hiking the trails in this region. A cap or hat with visor should also be considered.

Hunting Seasons

Hikers should be aware that, unlike the national park system, sport hunting is permitted on all public lands within the Adirondack and Catskill state parks. There are separate rules and seasons for each type of hunting (small game, waterfowl, and big game); but it is the big-game season, i.e. deer and bear, that is most likely to cause concern for hikers.

For those hikers who might be concerned, the following is a list of all big-game hunting seasons—running from approximately mid-September through early December.

Early Bear Season: Begins the first Saturday after the second Monday in September and continues for four weeks.

Archery Season (deer and bear): September 27 to opening of the regular season.

Muzzleloading Season (deer and bear): The seven days prior to the opening of regular season.

Regular Season: Next to last Saturday in October through the first Sunday in December.

During any of these open seasons, prudence dictates the wearing of at least one piece of brightly colored clothing, although the chance of actually encountering hunters on mountain trails is relatively small given that the game being pursued, and consequently the hunters themselves, do not favor the steeper mountain slopes. Although hunters might use portions of marked hiking trails as access, they recognize that hiker traffic along the marked trail frightens game animals so that their best chance of success is far from those areas frequented by hikers.

The Adirondack Mt. Club does not promote hunting as one of its organized activities, but it does recognize that sport hunting, when carried out in compliance with the game laws administered by the Dept. of Environmental Conservation, is a legitimate and necessary method of managing game populations. The harassment of hunters engaged in the legitimate pursuit of their sport is not appropriate. Suspected violations of the game laws should be reported to the nearest DEC Forest Ranger or Conservation Officer.

Emergency Procedures

An ounce of prevention is always worth a pound of cure, but if one is in need of emergency assistance, the DEC forest rangers are the first people to contact for help: Call Regions 5 and 6 Search and Rescue, Ray Brook (518) 891-0235.

If they cannot be contacted, then call the New York State Police (518-897-2000 in Ray Brook). They will use whatever means needed to contact persons able to help. Make sure that the person going for help has the above telephone numbers plus a complete written description of the type and exact location of the accident.

Off-Trail Hiking

Off-trail hiking in this region will mainly take the form of bush-whacking, although there are some unmarked, overgrown fishermen's trails that can be followed to certain remote ponds officially not reachable by trail. An unmarked trail that can be followed with a little caution is the Dobson Trail, which leaves the High Falls Truck Trail at 1.1 mi. to intersect the Plains Trail, giving the shortest route to High Falls. There are a few other trails, long abandoned, which can still be followed for a distance with somewhat more difficulty in overcoming blowdowns and beaver flooding. Two examples here, both of which can be followed with caution for several miles, are the trail across the Oswegatchie River from High Falls running over Greenleaf Mt., and the trail off the Hayes Brook Truck Trail that runs over a shoulder of East Mt.

For the seasoned hiker, the main interest in off-trail hiking is, however, authentic bushwhacking – going cross-country to a particular destination without benefit of trails of any kind. In this relatively isolated part of the Adirondacks with many remote and trailless areas, this is not a project to be undertaken lightly. Bush-whacking also differs in this region because of the relatively few open summits which are easy to bushwhack and from which a directional bearing may be made. As a consequence, most of the bushwhacks of interest in this region will lead to trailless headwater ponds.

With a lack of heights and other prominent field marks in which to take cross bearings, and with beaver flooding obstructing the way more often than not, it goes without saying that any bushwhacking in this area should be attempted only by those proficient in the use of map and compass and with an absolute minimum of four to a party at all times. Allowance, of course, has to be made for the magnetic declination of 12 to 14 degrees W which is present in this region. The bushwhacking party should try to use a base line as a hedge against a margin of error in reading the compass. Common base lines that are suitable in this region include marked trails, moderate-sized streams, and, of course, roads of all kinds.

Some of the trailless ponds occasionally reached by bushwhacking in this region are Otter Pond, also known locally as Big Otter Pond (from the Oswegatchie River), Indian Mt. Pond (from the Six Mile Creek Trail) and various ponds S of High Falls in the Five Ponds Wilderness Area. These latter bushwhacks should be undertaken with the utmost caution and after the maximum preparation has been made as they are located in the largest trailless area in New York, if not the entire Northeast.

Two of the isolated peaks described in this region can be bushwhacked entirely through Forest Preserve lands. They are St. Regis Mt. from St. Regis Pond and DeBar Mt. from Meacham Lake and Campsite. Long Pond Mt. in the St. Regis Canoe Area is also occasionally reached by bushwhack from the shores of Long Pond.

Canoe Routes

The northern region, because of its abundant waterways, is probably the premier area in the Adirondacks for canoeing. The routes over these waterways are usually relatively uncrowded and, as often as not, traverse a pristine habitat of towering conifers and extensive wetlands.

The many small rivers flowing northerly to the St. Lawrence River over the broad plateau that comprises the main portion of the region make exciting canoe routes when they are in the public domain. Some of the more prominent are the Oswegatchie River from Inlet, the Grass River from the DeGrasse State Forest, the Osgood River from Osgood Pond, and the St. Regis River from Everton Falls. The state is currently negotiating for a canoe route along the Raquette River from Piercefield to Seveys Corners.

An exciting new canoe route has been opened up on the Bog River near Horseshoe Lake. A long canoe carry connects the headwaters of the Bog and Oswegatchie Rivers. Recent state acquisition of land along the Grass River by NY Route 3 and the Yorkshire Conservation Easement lands make possible a canoe route on the upper portion of the Grass River. Care should be exercised in not trespassing on the portions of the river that remain private lands.

The multitude of ponds in the St. Regis Canoe Area can also be linked together with short carries for a truly unique canoeing experience. Two of the most noteworthy of these canoe routes which date back to the famous hotels of the last century are the Route of the Nine Carries and the Route of the Seven Carries. Both of these rely on different branches of the St. Regis River in proceeding from headwater pond to headwater pond. For further information on canoeing in the northern region, see Paul Jamieson and Donald Morris' excellent book *Adirondack Canoe Waters: North Flow*, published by ADK.

The Adirondack Mountain Club

The Adirondack Mountain Club (or ADK, the initials AMC having been claimed by the previously formed Appalachian Mountain Club) was organized in 1922 for the purpose of bringing together in a working unit a large number of people interested in the mountains, trails, camping, and forest conservation in New York State. A permanent club head-quarters was established, and with an increasing membership, club chapters were organized. The chapters are as follows:

Adirondak Loj (North Elba), Albany, Algonquin (Plattsburgh), Black River (Watertown), Cold River (Long Lake), Finger Lakes (Ithaca-

ADK's Adirondak Loj

ADK's Adirondack Headquarters & Information Center

Elmira), Genesee Valley (Rochester), Glens Falls, Hurricane Mt. (Keene), Iroquois (Utica), Keene Valley, Knickerbocker (New York City and vicinity), Lake Placid, Laurentian (Canton-Potsdam), Long Island, Mid-Hudson (Poughkeepsie), Mohican (Westchester and Putnam counties, NY, and Fairfield County, CT), New York (metropolitan area), Niagara Frontier (Buffalo), North Jersey (Bergen County), North Woods (Saranac Lake-Tupper Lake), Onondaga (Syracuse), Ramapo (Rockland and Orange counties), Schenectady, Shatagee Woods (Malone), and Susquehanna (Oneonta). In addition, there is an extensive membership-at-large.

Most chapters do not have qualifying requirements: a note to the Membership Assistant, Adirondack Mountain Club, 814 Goggins Road, Lake George, NY 12845-4117, will bring you information on membership in a local chapter (e.g., names and addresses of persons to be contacted) or details on membership-at-large. Persons joining a chapter, upon payment of their chapter dues, *ipso facto* become members of the club. Membership dues include a subscription to *Adirondac*, a bimonthly magazine; and discounts on ADK books and at ADK lodges. An application for membership is in the back of this book.

Members of the Adirondack Mountain Club have formulated the following creed, which reflects the theme of the club and its membership:

> We, the Adirondack Mountain Club, believe that the lands of the State constituting the Forest Preserve should be forever kept as wild forest lands in accordance with Article XIV, Section 1, of the New York State Constitution. We favor a program under the administration of the Department of Environmental Conservation (in the Adirondacks, pursuant to the Adirondack Park Agency policy) that will provide ample opportunities for outdoor recreation in a manner

consistent with the wild forest character of the Preserve. We favor acquisition of additional wild lands to meet the goals of the State Land Master Plans for watershed and wildlife protection and for recreation needs, and we support protection of the open-space character of appropriate private lands within the Adirondack and Catskill parks. We believe an informed public is essential to the well-being of the Preserve and the parks. We seek to accomplish measures that are consistent with this policy, and we oppose measures that are contrary thereto.

In the 1990s, approximately 22,000 "ADKers" enjoy the full spectrum of outdoor activities, including hiking, backpacking, canoeing (from floating on a pond to whitewater racing), rock climbing, cross-country skiing and snowshoeing. Most chapters have an active year-round outings schedule as well as regular meetings, sometimes including a meal, and programs featuring individuals ranging from chapter members to local and state officials. Many ADKers are also active in service work ranging from participation in search-and-rescue organizations to involvement in the ongoing debate over the best use of our natural resources and forest or wilderness lands, not only in the Adirondacks but also in their immediate localities.

ADK Facilities

ADK Information Center & Headquarters:

At the southernmost corner of the Park is the long log cabin that serves as ADK's Adirondack Park Information Center and Headquarters. The building, located just off exit 21 of I-87 ("the Northway")

about 0.2 mi. S on Route 9N, is open year-round. Hours: 1st weekend
in May to Columbus Day, Monday–Saturday, 8:30 a.m.–5 p.m.;
Tuesday after Columbus Day–1st weekend in May, Monday–Friday,
8:30 a.m.–4:30 p.m.

ADK staff at this facility provide information about hiking, canoeing, cross-country skiing, climbing and camping in the Adirondack
and Catskill parks. In addition, they host lectures, workshops, and
exhibits; sell publications and ADK logo items; and provide membership information. For further information, call or write ADK, 814
Goggins Rd., Lake George, NY 12845-4117 (telephone: 518-668-
4447). For information about ADK accommodations, see below.

High Peaks Information Center:

Located on the Heart Lake property near the trailheads for many
of the region's highest peaks, the High Peaks Information Center (HPIC)
offers backcountry and general Adirondack information, educational
displays, publications, some outdoor equipment, and trail snacks.

Adirondack Mountain Club Lodges:

The Adirondack Mountain Club, Inc., owns and operates two
lodges for overnight guests in the High Peaks Region. Johns Brook
Lodge is accessible only by foot, whereas Adirondak Loj can be
reached by car.

Johns Brooks Lodge: Johns Brook Lodge (JBL) is on the trail to
Mt. Marcy 5.1 mi. from Keene Valley and 3.5 mi. from the trailhead
at the Garden. The lodge is open to all comers for meals and lodging
daily from mid-June until Labor Day, during which it has a resident
staff, and weekends from Memorial Day weekend until late June and
the weekend after Labor Day until Columbus Day on a caretaker
basis. During the summer season, the hutmaster in charge will make

every effort to accommodate transients, but only reservations in advance will guarantee space in one of the two bunkrooms. Available all year long in the immediate vicinity of JBL are other accommodations owned by the Adirondack Mountain Club, Inc.: three lean-tos, and two cabins with cooking facilities—Winter Camp, housing 12, and Grace Camp, housing six. For further details and reservation information, contact Johns Brook Lodge, c/o Adirondak Loj, P.O. Box 867, Lake Placid, NY 12946.

Adirondak Loj: This facility (whose unusual spelling stems from the phonetic spelling system of Melvil Dewey, founder of the Lake Placid Club, which built the original structure), is 9 mi. by car from the village of Lake Placid. In addition to the Loj, the Adirondack Mountain Club owns the square mile of surrounding property, including all of Heart Lake and most of Mt. Jo. The Loj offers accommodations to all comers by the day or week, all year long, either in private bedrooms or in bunkrooms. Other accommodations include cabins, lean-tos with fireplaces, and numerous tent sites, for which nominal charges are made. Basic camping supplies may be purchased at the High Peaks Information Center located at the entrance to the parking lot at the Loj. A parking fee is charged to nonmembers not registered at the Loj or using the lean-tos and tent sites.

Several cross-country ski trails are located on the property and on nearby Forest Preserve land. This extensive network is a center of much wintertime activity. Snowshoers find much territory in which to enjoy their particular sport.

Of special interest at Adirondak Loj is a Nature Museum where one may find specimens of mosses, lichens, birds' nests, rocks and other Adirondack features. A modest library is available to help those who wish to identify their own samples.

A ranger-naturalist program is offered during the summer months. The leader conducts walks along a special nature trail and furnishes talks and slide shows on conservation and natural history topics. The latter are generally conducted in a scenic outdoor amphitheatre especially constructed for this purpose.

For full information about reservations, rates, or activities, address the Manager at Adirondak Loj, P.O. Box 867, Lake Placid, NY 12946 (telephone: 518-523-3441).

NEAL BURDICK, Forest Preserve Series Editor
PETER V. O'SHEA, JR.

Long Lake Section

A small cluster of interesting trails is grouped around the hamlet of Long Lake. These trails and loops travel generally through a handsome, mature forest of mixed hardwoods and conifers as they lead to the shores of some of the large, sprawling wild lakes of this area: Raquette Lake, Lake Eaton, and Lake Lila. In addition there is a fairly sharp ascent up a modest-sized mountain to overlook the shore of Long Lake itself. The trails are located mainly in the Sargent Pond Wild Forest. The outlying Lake Lila-Frederica Mt. trail to the north is also placed in this chapter. Included in the first edition but now omitted is the Campsite snowmobile trail linking Lake Eaton and Forked Lake Campsite, which has been abandoned and which is now encumbered by blow-down in a number of places. The one ascent is to the top of Owls Head Mt., one of the area's highest eminences. There is a DEC forest ranger located at Long Lake and there are state campsites at Lake Eaton and Forked Lake. The area is covered by the following topographic maps: Raquette Lake 7.5 x 15-min. and Long Lake 15-min. series.

Short Hike:

Sargent Pond Loop – *5.0 mi. An easy woods jaunt past four lovely ponds. A 1.5 mi. walk on a public road is required to complete the loop if a second car is not available.*

Moderate Hike:

Owls Head Mt. – *6.2–mi. round trip. Except for a difficult pitch just before the summit, this is a not-too-difficult climb providing outstanding views.*

(1) Sargent Pond Loop   Page Map

This is a red-marked DEC circuit that can be made by parking two cars at different trailheads 1.5 mi. apart on the North Point Rd. The loop passes the shores of three charming Adirondack lakes.

Trailhead: *Access is from the North Point Rd. at Deerland, which is approximately 3.0 mi. S of Long Lake village on NY 30 and NY 28. Go R on the North Point Rd. and proceed W approximately 6.3 mi. to the first marked trailhead seen on the L. Park one vehicle here. The second trailhead, where the other vehicle should be parked, is 1.5 mi. farther W on North Point Rd. The loop begins at the* **second** *trailhead.*

The trail goes through a forest of mostly mature hardwoods as it proceeds on a rolling course to reach the shores of Grassy Pond in 1.3 mi. Grassy Pond is a small conifer-ringed pond with grass-like sedges lining the shore on one side. Sharp hills envelop it on two sides.

The trail traverses many small, spring-fed creeks and continues undulating under an impressive canopy of yellow birch and hemlock until it reaches a junction at 2.0 mi. The trail R leads to Tioga Point on Raquette Lake, reaching Lower Sargent Pond in 0.1 mi.

The trail now begins a gradual ascent to the L among large sugar maples. At 2.8 mi. it passes Middle Pond, a tiny kettle pond

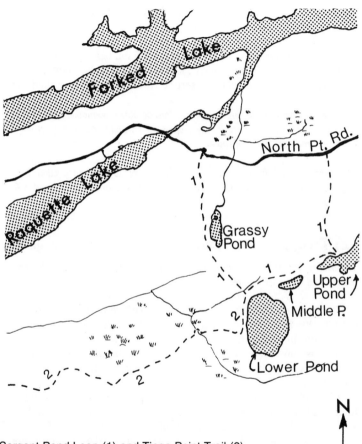

Sargent Pond Loop (1) and Tioga Point Trail (2)
Based on Raquette Lake & Blue Mt. quadrangles

surrounded by wetlands off to the R. The course now is rolling to a junction with Upper Sargent Pond at 3.7 mi.

The trail now turns L and continues 1.3 mi. to reach the first trailhead on North Pond Road at a point 1.5 mi. before the second trailhead. If there is only one car, it is a pleasant walk along a little-used winding road to reach the second trailhead and the parked car.

Trail in winter: May be skied in winter. Considerable snowmobile use (from Long Lake) on weekends occasionally. Depending on weather conditions spring-fed creeks may be devoid of snow.

Distances: Second trailhead to Grassy Pond, 1.3 mi.; to first trail junction, 2.0 mi.; to second trail junction, 3.7 mi.; to North Point Road and first trailhead, 5.0 mi. (8.0 km).

(2) Tioga Point Trail   Page Map

Trailhead: This trail begins at a junction at 2.0 mi. on the Sargent Pond Loop. A red marked trail goes R here.

The trail descends sharply to cross a creek on a wooden bridge at 0.1 mi. This is the outlet of Sargent Pond. Lower Sargent is circular with medium-sized spruce lining its bank. The wooden dam at the outlet was constructed in connection with lumbering activities in the past. The wooden bridge has been occasionally washed out by flooding in the past.

The trail now climbs a ridge and crosses over it until it descends to an old beaver flow at 0.8 mi. The trail crosses another wetland at 1.8 mi. At 2.1 mi. it crosses the edge of an extensive spruce-fir swamp with occasional majestic white pine at its edge. The trail then rises moderately to pass through red and white pines before reaching Tioga Point at 3.2 mi. The abundant lean-tos and manicured grassy areas here are in sharp contrast to the silent majestic forest passed through in reaching this point. The site receives heavy use during the summer from boat campers from the Raquette Lake village area.

Trail in winter: *This trail may be skied in winter, despite being narrow and steep in places.*

Distances: *To Lower Sargent Pond, 0.1 mi.; to Tioga Point, 3.2 mi.*

(3) Owls Head Mt. Trail Page Map

The red-marked trail to the top of Owls Head Mt. starts at the outskirts of Long Lake village and ascends one of the isolated peaks of this region, providing a panoramic view of the surrounding area.

Trailhead: *Access is achieved by taking NY 30 N from the center of Long Lake to Endion Rd. on the L at the edge of the village. It is 1.6 mi. on Endion Rd. to the trailhead on the R.*

There are two more or less parallel trails at the outset. The trail to the R is marked as a snowmobile trail. The L trail immediately begins a steep climb under large hemlock and yellow birch. At 0.5 mi. it levels off as sugar maple becomes prominent. The snowmobile trail comes in on the R; the two trails now run concurrently. At 0.8 mi. the snowmobile trail makes a slight detour R before rejoining the hiking trail after a short distance.

At 1.1 mi. the trail reaches a junction with DEC signs. The trail R is the abandoned Lake Eaton Campsite-Forked Lake Campsite Trail to Lake Eaton. The Owls Head Mt. Trail proceeds straight; it is now marked with both red hiking trail markers and the larger red snowmobile trail markers, since the abandoned Lake Eaton Campsite-Forked Lake Campsite Trail and the Owls Head Trail are

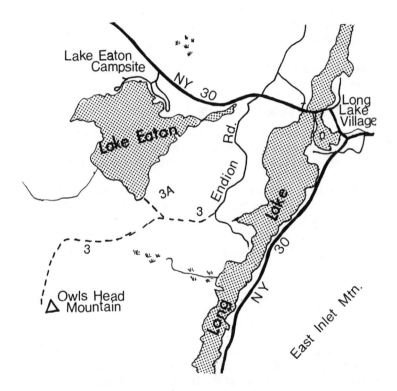

Owls Head Mt. (3) and Lake Eaton (3A) trails
Based on Raquette Lake & Blue Mt. quadrangles

simultaneous for the next 0.3 mi. To add somewhat to the confusion, an occasional yellow snowmobile trail marker is encountered. These were used by DEC until being replaced recently by the red markers. The signs at this and subsequent junctions are clear, however, so the variations in trail marker colors should not prove troublesome.

At 1.2 mi. a recessed sign is seen on the R. This marks the junction with the Lake Eaton Trail (trail 3A), a short, sporadically marked trail that leads to the shore of Lake Eaton. The Owls Head Mt. Trail continues under a canopy of hemlocks with occasional telephone poles still standing as testimony to the manned fire tower that once stood on top of Owls Head Mt.

At 1.4 mi. the trail reaches another marked DEC junction. The abandoned Lake Eaton Campsite-Forked Lake Campsite Trail goes L to Forked Lake in 8.2 mi. while the Owls Head Mt. Trail again continues straight. Small red trail markers point the way; the red and yellow snowmobile disks indicate the trail to Forked Lake.

At 1.8 mi. a steep ravine is passed on the L. Spruce now begins to come into the canopy. At 2.0 mi. the trail begins to climb, getting rockier and steeper at 2.5 mi. Another ravine is passed on the L and large beech is now present. At 2.7 mi. the way is encumbered slightly by blowdown until at 2.8 mi. the remnants of the fire observer's cabin are passed in an open glade underneath the pinnacle of Owls Head.

The trail now begins a very steep scramble to the top, starting to rise just past the open glade. This last ascent is somewhat strenuous and may entail the use of the hands in climbing. Finally at 3.1 mi. the summit with its small open area surrounded by conifers is attained. From the 2780-foot peak Owls Head Pond is seen immediately below with good views of Raquette Lake and Forked Lake to the SW. The hazy summit of Blue Mt. is seen just E of S, while Kempshall Mt. looms ahead in the distance. The 14 miles of Long Lake itself, so close by, are mostly hidden from view.

Trail in winter: This trail is not suitable for cross-country skiing in winter due to steepness of terrain.

Distances: Endion Road to jct. with campsite trail, 1.1 mi.; to jct. with unmarked Lake Eaton Trail on R, 2.1 mi.; to summit of Owls Head Mt., 3.1 mi. (5.0 km).

(3A) Lake Eaton Trail Page Map

Trailhead: The short, mostly unmarked trail to Lake Eaton begins on the R at a currently unmarked junction at 1.2 mi. on the Owls Head Mt. trail.

The trail proceeds through a mixed, mostly mature forest, reaching the shores of Lake Eaton in 0.4 mi. (At this point there is an unmarked trail junction with the abandoned Lake Eaton Campsite-Forked Lake Campsite Trail.) A small sandy beach is present here, along with a canopy of large conifers – mainly white pine. These conifers circle the rim of the lake for a good part of its circumference. Across the lake from this site is the developed DEC Lake Eaton campsite.

Trail in winter: Generally not practical for winter use due to brevity and to steep terrain on trail that leads to trailhead.

Distance: Owls Head Mt. Trail to Lake Eaton, 0.4 mi. (0.6 km).

(4) Lake Lila–Frederica Mt. Trail Page Map

This blue-marked trail provides access to the largest lake wholly contained in the Forest Preserve, while traversing what was once one of the largest private parks in the Adirondacks: Nehasane Park.

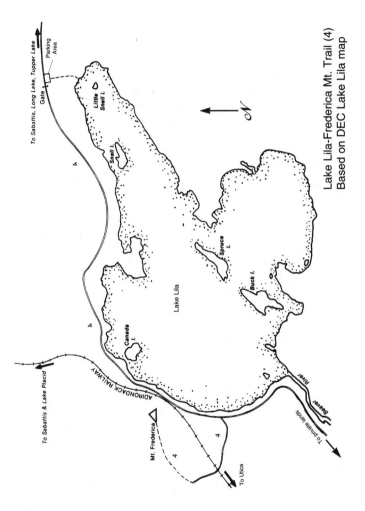

Lake Lila-Frederica Mt. Trail (4)
Based on DEC Lake Lila map

Trailhead: *Access is from NY 30 at the marked turn for Sabattis. This is approximately 11.5 mi. S of the village of Tupper Lake and approximately 10.0 mi. N of the village of Long Lake. The access road to Lake Lila is on the L at 7.7 mi. on the Sabattis Rd. Marked with a DEC sign, this is locally known as the Charley Pond Rd. A DEC parking lot and metal barrier barring any further travel by unauthorized vehicles are at 5.8 mi. The trail starts immediately past the barrier.*

The trail is mainly level with occasional spruce and pine present until it starts to rise at 0.7 mi. Medium-sized hardwoods are now seen. At 1.5 mi., it comes to the shores of Lake Lila (at the parking lot a short 0.3 mi. yellow-marked canoe carry also provides access to the lake). Several of the forested islands of the lake can be observed here, as can the low hill encircling the lake on the W.

The trail now starts to run along the lakeshore with occasional large white pine present. At 1.9 mi. Harrington Brook is crossed as it empties into the lake. At 2.6 mi. a log road goes off R to reach the old railroad station of the Remsen-Lake Placid line. The building was still standing in 1984. At 2.8 mi. a lean-to is seen on the L at the lakeshore.

At 3.0 mi., at a junction, the trail to Frederica Mt. goes R. (Straight ahead the site of the old Nehasane Lodge is reached in 0.2 mi. This short trail is marked with yellow markers. Nehasane Lodge, one of the "great camps" of the Adirondacks, was destroyed by the DEC in 1984 in compliance with the State Land Master Plan.) At 3.2 mi. it starts to rise through large hemlock and sugar maple. The trail then descends with yellow birch and red maple saplings lining its sides.

At 3.5 mi. the old railroad grade is crossed. The railroad bed is not part of the Lake Lila Primitive Area at present and is used by snow-mobilers in winter. This is why there are "no unauthorized motor vehicles" signs on the sides of the tracks at the Primitive Area roadway.

At 3.6 mi. a wooden bridge crosses over a creek with an old beaver pond on the R. The trail continues to the Frederica Mt. trail sign on the R at 3.8 mi. The trail then ascends through a mixed forest of softwoods and hardwoods to the overlook on Frederica Mt. at 4.4 mi. The remnants of the privately erected lean-to which was demolished by the DEC can still be noticed here.

From the top of Frederica Mt. an unequaled view of Lake Lila below and all the surrounding wilderness area may be had. Viewing all these verdant acres today, it is hard to believe that the entire Nehasane Park together with the adjoining hamlet of Sabattis (then called Long Lake West) was severely burned by the disastrous forest fire of 1908.

Trail in winter: This trail is suitable for cross-country skiing to the base of Frederica Mt., a distance of 3.8 mi. from the parking lot. A further 5.8 mi. will have to be skied from the Sabattis Rd. if the access road is not plowed (it usually isn't) and if parking can be accomplished on the Sabattis Rd.

Distances: Parking lot to the base of Frederica Mt., 3.8 mi.; to summit of Frederica Mt., 4.4 mi. (7.0 km).

Tupper Lake Section

A varied group of interesting trails is centered around the village of Tupper Lake, one of the largest in Adirondack Park. The village, once the core of the lumbering and wood-using industry in the Adirondacks, today shares this industry with tourism and recreation.

The mostly disjunct trails here in many cases join some of the area's numerous ponds and lakes, occasionally forming a chain linking these glacial relics to each other. Other trails ascend to the top of the region's isolated mountains, offering stunning views of the pond-strewn sprawling woodlands unfurled below.

Some of the forests through which the various trails pass are themselves quite spectacular. Probably no other part of the Adirondack Park (with the exception of the remote Five Pond Wilderness located nearby) possesses such an abundance and variety of old-growth forest as do some of the woodlands here. Especially noteworthy in this regard are the forests along the Ampersand Mt. and Middle Saranac Lake trails and those on the Otter Hollow and Floodwood Loop.

The Wawbeek Truck Trail and the Wawbeek-Lead Pond Link Trail from the first edition have been omitted as they are now legs of the Deer Pond Loop. The Rollins Pond Trail has been deleted due to serious beaver flooding.

DEC ranger stations are located in the village of Tupper Lake and in the adjoining hamlet of Piercefield in St. Lawrence County. Two very large DEC campsites are located at Fish Creek Pond and Rollins Pond.

This area is covered by the following USGS topographical map: Upper Saranac Lake 7.5 x 15-min. series.

Short Hike:

Saranac Lake Trail – 1.2–mi. round trip. A nearly level walk to a pleasant spot on the shore of Middle Saranac Lake.

Moderate Hike:

Ampersand Mt. – 5.6–mi. round trip. A delightful woods walk followed by some steep sections, Ampersand provides one of the finest views in the Adirondacks.

Harder Hike:

Otter Hollow Loop – 10.6 mi. This hike is difficult not because of its terrain—mostly gently undulating through mixed forest with many ponds to view—but because of its distance.

Trail Described	Total Miles (one way)	Page
Big Trout Lake Trail	2.2	47
Mt. Arab Trail	1.0	49
Panther Mt. Trail	0.6	52
Saranac Lake Trail	0.6	54
Ampersand Mt. Trail	2.8	54
Deer Pond Loop	7.3	58
Lead Pond Trail	2.1	59
Fernow Plantation Trail	1.1	60
Floodwood Loop	9.0	61
Otter Hollow Loop	10.6	63

(5) Big Trout Lake Trail   Page Map

This red-marked DEC snowmobile trail goes through the Horse-shoe Lake Wild Forest, giving access to a deep two-tiered lake

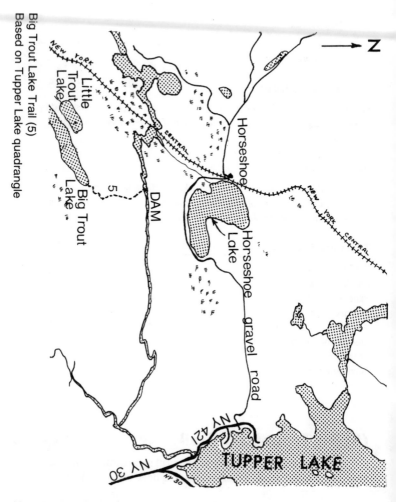

Big Trout Lake Trail (5)
Based on Tupper Lake quadrangle

providing habitat for both brook trout and lake trout.

Trailhead: *Access is from the Horseshoe Lake Road (NY 421), 6.4 mi. S of the Tupper Lake DEC boat launching site. NY 421 turns W here off NY 30 and proceeds 6 mi. to the end of the pavement. The dirt road on the L, 1 mi. past the end of the pavement has now been upgraded so that the 0.8 mi. to the Upper Dam can be driven with care. Cars may be parked here at the side of the road to begin the hike.*

The trail begins to climb among mature hardwoods shortly after crossing the dam. At 1.1 mi. the crest of a hill is reached after a steady ascent. This hill is crowned with majestic mature beech, apparently in good health. A steep ridge is viewed on the L across a swale; it is adorned with magnificent white pine and hemlock. At 1.4 mi. the trail reaches Big Trout Lake, long and narrow with white pine fringing its shore. This isolated body of water received its name from the large lake trout lurking in its depths.

Trail in winter: *Suitable for cross-country skiing from extension of County Route 421 to end of trail. Steep in area near end. It is 0.8 mi. from Route 421 to Dam.*

Distances: *Trail in summer: Dam to Big Trout Pond, 1.4 mi.; Ski trail: Route 421 to Big Trout Pond, 2.2 mi. (3.5 km).*

(6) Mt. Arab Trail

Page Map

The Mt. Arab Trail, marked in red, leads to a closed fire tower that was still standing in 1992.

With recent state acquisition of a conservation easement from Yorkshire Timber Company, access to this attractive mountain has been virtually assured. A small section of the trail just before Forest Preserve land still belongs to another timber company, but this

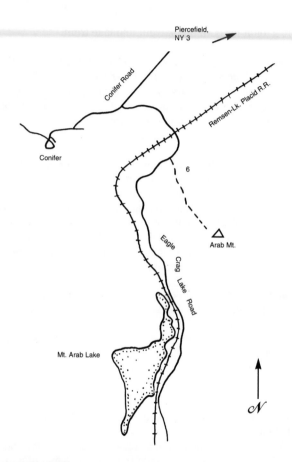

Mt. Arab Trail (6)
Base map is Piercefield quadrangle

should not interfere with public access to the summit.

Trailhead: *Access is off the Conifer Rd., which intersects NY 3 approximately 4.0 mi. W of Tupper Lake and 10.4 mi. E of Sevey's Corners—the intersection of NY 3 and NY 56. Take the Conifer Rd. 1.8 mi S to the Eagle Crag Lake Rd. on the L. Take this road 0.9 mi. to the trailhead on the L. Look carefully for signs here—the official DEC sign is frequently missing. The start is 0.3 mi. after crossing the tracks of the old Remsen–Lake Placid railroad.*

After a stand of medium-sized hardwoods at the outset, the trail begins to rise immediately. At 0.3 mi. it enters the Forest Preserve, having traversed private lands.

The trail continues the steep climb until 0.8 mi., where it begins to level off amidst large outcrops of granite. It then begins to circle and finally reaches the summit at 1.0 mi. The usual growth of stunted red spruce mantles the 2545-ft. summit here, just as it does the other low mountains of this area of the Adirondacks. Mountain ash is also present on the summit, which was severely burned over in the early years of the century.

In the center of the small clearing at the top stands the abandoned fire tower and observer's cabin. The steps of the fire tower were removed in 1993. Mt. Arab Lake and Eagle Crag Lake are nearby to the S by SE, while Mt. Matumbla, the highest in St. Lawrence County, is directly N. To the N by NE, Raquette Pond and Tupper Lakevillage can be clearly seen, while due E Mt. Morris looms ahead. N by NW Moosehead Mountain can be seen. The summits of these surrounding mountains are all on private land or blocked by private land and are therefore unavailable to the general hiking public. All can be seen to be of approximately the same elevation as Mt. Arab.

Trail in winter: *This trail is not suitable for skiing in winter due to steepness of terrain.*

Distance: *road to summit: 1.0 mi. (1.6 km).*

(7) Panther Mt. Trail

Page Map

This short, steep, red-marked trail climbs steadily to the peak of an isolated, moderate-sized mountain between the villages of Tupper Lake and Saranac Lake.

Trailhead: *Access is from NY 3, approximately 1.6 mi. E of the junction of NY 3 and NY 30 at Wawbeek Corners. The trailhead sign and access is on the L side of NY 3; cars should be parked to the R (S) of the road at the small parking lot for Panther Road Fishing Access.*

The trail starts across NY 3 and immediately begins to ascend through a mixed mature forest of beech and hemlock. At 0.3 mi. hemlock becomes dominant with little undergrowth present. This sparsity of low-growing vegetation and the high humidity are both typical of hemlock forests. Shortly afterward, sugar maple begin to appear and a resultant lush understory of striped maple also appears. This is due to increased sunlight.

At 0.4 mi., scattered white birch begin to appear. This usually denotes the scene of a past fire. At 0.6 mi. the trail reaches the exposed rock summit of Panther Mt. USGS markers are scattered among the blueberry bushes sprawling along the summit. The view immediately beneath the mountain is obstructed by trees; on the horizon, however, Tupper Lake and County Line Island are clearly seen to the W. The High Peaks can be discerned at a distance on clear days to the SE.

Trail in winter: *Not suitable due to steepness of terrain.*

Distance: *NY 3 to summit, 0.6 mi. (1.0 km).*

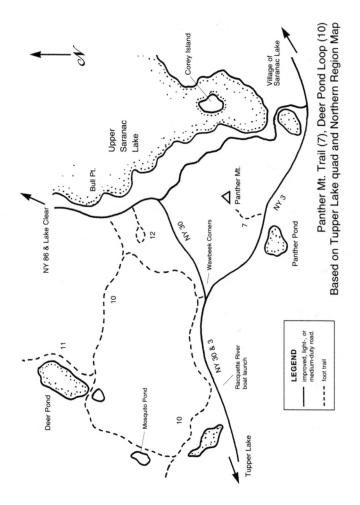

Panther Mt. Trail (7), Deer Pond Loop (10)
Based on Tupper Lake quad and Northern Region Map

(8) Saranac Lake Trail

Page Map

This short, attractive trail arrives at the underdeveloped shoreline of Middle Saranac Lake after proceeding through a charming forest of mature evergreens.

Trailhead: Access is from the Ampersand Mt. Trail parking lot on the N side of NY 3, 7.0 mi. E of the junction of NY 3 and NY 30, and 8.0 mi. W of the village of Saranac Lake.

The trail begins by descending a bank at the parking area on rough wooden stairs. It then enters a mature forest primarily of hemlock, spruce and yellow birch with occasional beech and sugar maple. The forest appears to be intermediate in kind between the moist spruce flat type and the much drier beech-maple type.

The trail proceeds along the side of a knoll until it passes just to the R of a swamp at 0.5 mi. Shortly thereafter at 0.6 mi., the shores of Middle Saranac Lake are reached. There are several picnic tables and a fireplace here. Cedar, tamarack and white pine are now added to the cast of trees. A wide beach is on the R; the shoreline vista at this point shows the lakeshore heavily wooded in all directions, with signs of man practically nonexistent.

Trail in winter: Suitable for short ski tour.

Distance: NY 3 to Middle Saranac Lake, 0.6 mi. (1.0 km).

(9) Ampersand Mt. Trail

Page Map

The trail up Ampersand Mt., being just outside the boundaries included in the guide, was not described in the first edition. However, the popularity of this trail along with the splendid view from its

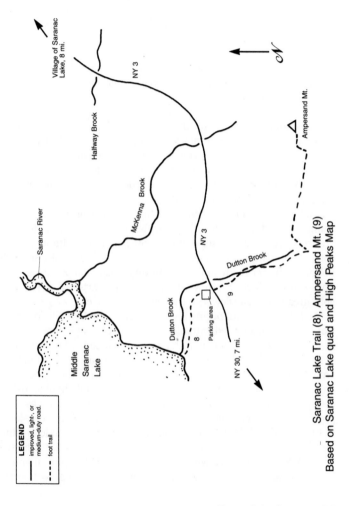

LEGEND

— improved, light-, or medium-duty road.

- - - foot trail

Village of Saranac Lake, 8 mi.

NY 3

Halfway Brook

Saranac River

McKenna Brook

Middle Saranac Lake

Dutton Brook

Dutton Brook

NY 3

Ampersand Mt.

9

8

Parking area

NY 30, 7 mi.

N

Saranac Lake Trail (8), Ampersand Mt. (9)
Based on Saranac Lake quad and High Peaks Map

commanding peak and the magnificence of the forest traversed warrant its inclusion in this second edition.

Trailhead: Access is directly across NY 3 from the trailhead to the Middle Saranac Lake Trail, 8.1 mi. west of the village of Saranac Lake and 7.3 mi. east of Wawbeek Corners.

The trail is fairly level for the first mile crossing Dutton Brook and a wet area at 0.8 mi. Several small knolls are crossed but very little actual climbing is done for this first stretch. The attraction here is the forest itself – a classic example of what is designated as a hemlock-northern hardwood forest by the state's Natural Heritage Program jointly sponsored by DEC and the SUNY College of Environmental Science and Forestry. Towering sentinels of hemlock are complemented by occasional equally large specimens of yellow birch and somewhat smaller sugar maple. Striped maple with its handsome green bark is prominent in the understory, as is the sprawling hobblebush ever ready to trip an unwary hiker who proceeds off trail. The ground is literally strewn with a covering carpet of sorrel, goldthread, and starflower to the extent the eye can see.

At 1.2 mi. the trail begins its steep rise to the top. The lower slopes here are adorned with old growth beech-maple forest with much of the beech component having succumbed to beech bark scale disease. Although equally imposing, this designated type of old-growth forest is in a number of ways different from the preceding one. A conifer component is missing here, and while hobblebush is ever-present in the understory, striped maple is not nearly as prevalent being replaced mainly by honeysuckle and an occasional red-berry elder with striking purplish buds very noticeable in winter. The forest floor is festooned mostly with a layer of wood, Christmas and oak fern augmented with occasional false Solomon seal and Indian cucumber root. As is indicative of all truly old-growth forest, small openings are scattered throughout. These two stands have been prominently highlighted in New York State's Natural Heritage Program and give a vivid brief glimpse of what the original forest was like before being altered by man.

At 1.6 mi. the trail twists and veers right as it comes upon an opening with an old foundation present. This is the remnant of the fire observer's cabin that once stood on this spot. Walter Rice, one of the observers who dwelt here, is commemorated by a plaque up on the peak of the mountain.

After the old clearing, the trail gets quite steep and eroded in places. Some scrambling is required. Most of the approximately 1800 foot vertical elevation rise is attained here. At 2.5 mi. huge cliffs of bedrock and talus are passed just before the trail breaks into the open. White birch is prominent here, reflecting the fire that denuded the summit. Red spruce was formerly abundant but many have been killed by acid deposition. White cedar growing near the top adds a curious contrast here.

Follow yellow markers on the open rock for the last few hundred yards to the pinnacle at 2.7 mi. The view on top is wonderful, from privately owned Ampersand Lake below to the wild Seward Range in the foreground and Whiteface Mt. and the McKenzie Range in the far background to the north. While reflecting on what wildlife wonders may be still hidden in the remote and rugged Seward Range, consider also 19th-century Verplanck Colvin and his intrepid crew who were responsible for the controlled fire that burnt the top of this peak.

Trail in winter: *Not suitable due to steepness of terrain.*

Distances: *NY 3 to old clearing, 1.6 mi.; 2.7 mi. (4.3 km) to top.*

(10) Deer Pond Loop

Page Map, p. 53

This rather lengthy loop, marked as a ski trail by DEC, has been created out of several shorter trails that were listed in the first edition of this guide.

Trailhead: *Access is from the western side of NY 3 approximately 1 mi. N of the Raquette River Boat Launch and 0.6 mi. S of Wawbeek Corners where NY 30 & NY 3 part.*

The trail starts at a parking area on the old Wawbeek Road at the point described above. Follow the yellow ski disks and begin by going around a gated barrier on a former truck trail. The gate is recessed and is at the far end of a short jeep road loop. Look carefully.

The first 1.2 mi. along the old truck trail is quite flat with some truly majestic white pine lining the route in places. At 1.2 mi. veer L at a jct. with another trail coming in from Bull Point on NY 30 (this jct. is 0.7 mi. from NY 30).

The trail continues mostly level through flats lined with small regenerating conifers until a spruce-fir swamp is crossed on a 200-yd. corduroy platform. At 2.1 mi. the trail rises rather sharply as it ascends a ridge. The trail here is narrow as it goes up and down several knobs. Glacial erratics are strewn liberally across the landscape with a steep cliff looming over the trail on the R. Finally at 2.9 mi. a trail junction is reached on a ridge top overlooking Deer Pond in the distance. Take the L here; the trail R is the start of the Lead Pond trail.

The trail descends from the junction to cross the end of Deer Pond at a neck between the pond and an enlarged beaver flow to the L. Deer Pond is noted locally for its excellent smallmouth bass fishing. Another ridge clothed with mature specimens of sugar maple and ∙ yellow birch is then slowly climbed.

At 3.9 mi. the trail descends to Mosquito Pond. This tiny glacial pond is encircled by a mat of sedges and heath plants which keep growing year by year. In a relatively short time a boreal wetland will occupy the spot where the pond is today. The trail climbs again and then descends to cross the outlet of a beaver pond at 4.4 mi.

The trail crosses yet another ridge, this one with a moderate gradient, before reaching the Old Wawbeek Rd. at 4.8 mi. The Norway spruce encountered on this low ridge were a part of the many plantations laid out in this area at the turn of the century by Bernhard Fernow, the father of American forestry. They persist today, slowly succumbing to the ravages of age and completely surrounded by a natural forest comprised solely of native species.

Turn L on Old Wawbeek Rd. and follow this nearly level grade back to the beginning point at 7.3 mi.

Trail in Winter: *Marked as a ski trail but narrow and twisting in places, with a few steep descents. The wooden corduroy may also prove difficult to ski over on occasion.*

Distances: *Trailhead to 1st junction, 1.2 mi.; to second jct., 2.9 mi.; to Deer Pond, 3.0 mi.; to Mosquito Pond, 3.9 mi.; to Old Wawbeek Rd., 4.8 mi.; to beginning of Loop, 7.3 mi. (11.7 km).*

(11) Lead Pond Trail   Map: L-7

Trailhead: *Before the designation of the Deer Pond Loop the Lead Pond Trail was a rather lengthy round-trip hike. It now starts at the ridge-top junction at mile 2.9 on the Deer Pond Loop.*

The trail descends to the shore of Deer Pond following red snowmobile disks (there are sporadic yellow ski disks here). A nice informal campsite overlooks the large pond. The trail then begins to undulate as it crosses several small knolls while paralleling the lake shore to the left. Some of the hemlock and yellow birch encountered here are quite impressive. The outlet of a conifer swamp is then crossed. The trail is well marked here but brushy in places with the presence of beavers intermittently noted – in some places, at considerable distances from the shores of the lake.

The trail leaves the lake and descends into an extensive conifer swamp. This swamp, known locally as Deer Pond Marsh, is a mixed wetland with solid stands of tamarack and black spruce.

At 1.1 mi. the old path (formerly a trail) that leads to Rollins Pond Campsite comes in on the R. Frequent flooding along the length of the trail has limited its use at times of flooding to a bushwhack.

The trail continues, following a generally level course to Lead Pond at 2.1 mi. The isolated pond, encircled by a bog mat and small conifers, is partially in Forest Preserve and partially on private land.

Trail in Winter: *Can be used as a cross-country ski trail with caution: the way is narrow, twisting, and has brush encroaching in a number of areas.*

Distances: *Deer Pond Loop Junction to Lead Pond, 2.1 mi. (3.4 km).*

(12) Fernow Plantation Trail Map: M-8

This short loop trail goes through one of the earliest state plantations in New York. These early forest plantations, although a curious anomaly today, played a part in reforesting the Adirondacks after the disastrous forest fires at the turn of the century. Marked by red DEC disks, this one was started in 1900 under the direction of Bernhard Fernow, who many consider one of the fathers of modern forestry.

Trailhead: *Access is on the W side of NY 30 approximately 0.3 mi. N of Wawbeek Corners, where NY 3 and NY 30 join.*

The trail immediately enters the forest, arriving at a trail register at 0.1 mi. Large, almost mature planted white pine and Norway spruce dominate the canopy here. At 0.3 mi., a large glacial erratic is encountered as the loop takes the R turn. It continues on a mostly level grade skirting the boundary of private land, continuing through the mature conifers, with little evidence of undergrowth except for a luxurious carpet of oxalis blanketing the forest floor in spring. At 0.8 mi., the loop is rejoined and the trail then proceeds back to NY 30 at 1.1 mi.

Trail in winter: *Suitable for a short ski tour.*

Distance: *NY 30 trailhead to return, 1.1 mi. (1.8 km).*

(13) Floodwood Loop

Map: M-6

This is a rather lengthy loop, linking some of the myriad glacial ponds in an entrancing region of alternating ridges and water – both a legacy of the receding glacier that once mantled the area. To add to the allure, much of the forest crowning the ridges is quite imposing— some of it appears to be truly first growth.

Trailhead: *The trail starts at the Fish Creek Ponds Campsite which is located on the L 5.5 mi. N of Wawbeek Corners on NY 30. A gate is on the R opposite campsite number twenty-three 0.2 mi. inside the campsite entrance. Begin here.*

Follow the red disks around the gate and make a sharp R at 0.1 mi. The path straight ahead also turns R and is the return leg of the Loop.

The way is marked by the splendid specimens of hemlock and yellow birch so prevalent in this region. Majestic red spruce is also present but some of it appears to be succumbing to unknown ravages (acid deposition is suspected by some). The trail makes a moderate ascent up a glacial knoll as it arrives at the first canoe carry at 0.9 mi. Fish Creek is to the L, Follensby Clear Pond on the R. The latter is one of the area's largest lakes and is adorned with a number of pine-clad islands.

The trail proceeds through a spruce swamp for a short distance and then rolls on to make a sharp L and then another L to reflect the contour of one of the bays of the aptly named Horseshoe Pond. The next canoe carry is at 2.6 mi.: atop a ridge after the outlet of Little Polliwog Pond, the carry to that tiny glacial pool goes off to the L. At 2.9 mi. a canoe carry going from Little Polliwog Pond to Polliwog Pond is encountered.

At 3.7 mi. the red-marked trail turns L on the canoe carry from Middle Pond to Polliwog Pond. To the right it is a short way to sprawling Polliwog Pond whose sentinel white pines have played host to nesting osprey in the recent past. At 4.0 mi. a R is made as the yellow canoe carry discs go straight ahead to Middle Pond. The trail arrives at the Floodwood Rd. at 4.2 mi.

The trail goes L on Floodwood Rd. along Middle Pond until 5.2 mi. where it goes L and again re-enters the forest. The trail now undulates as it crosses a wet spot spanned by a wooden bridge before coming to the intersection with yet another yellow marked canoe carry. Go R here; the way L goes to Middle Pond.

At 6.3 mi. turn L following the red discs; the yellow canoe carry arrives at Floodwood Pond in 400 ft. At 6.6 mi. the Otter Hollow Loop Cross-over is a short link crossing Fish Creek to connect the Floodwood Loop and the Otter Hollow Loop (trail 14). Trail continues over rolling ridges with Little Square Pond on the R.

At 8.5 mi. the final canoe carry is crossed. Fish Creek is on the R while the carry to the L goes to Follensby Clear Pond. The trail proceeds through a forest of pioneer white and grey birch then makes a sharp L to reach the point of origin at 9.0 mi.

Trail in Winter: *This trail is ideally suited for cross-country skiing. The magnificent old-growth forest traversed with a constant understory of hobblebush* adds to the allure of the trip. The glacial knolls in the two miles before Floodwood Rd. are more frequent and steeper than at the start and the trail is rather narrow throughout. Snowmobile use is occasionally heavy. The campground road is plowed to the caretaker's cabin (1.0 mi. inside entrance) in winter and no fee is charged after November.

Distances: Fish Creek campsite trailhead to Follensby Clear Pond, 0.9 mi.; Little Polliwog Pond, 2.6 mi.; Polliwog Pond, 2.9 mi.; Middle Pond, 3.7 mi.; Floodwood Rd., 4.2 mi.; Floodwood Pond, 6.3 mi.; Otter Hollow Loop Cross-over, 6.6 mi.; return to trailhead, 9.0 mi. (14.4 km).

(14) Otter Hollow Loop   Map: L-6

Trailhead: The Otter Hollow Loop begins in the Fish Creek Ponds Campsite on NY 30, 5.5 mi. N of Wawbeek Corners and links an assortment of glacial ponds under a towering arboreal canopy. The start is on the R opposite campsite #104, 1.1 mi. inside the camp entrance. The large lake here is Square Pond.

The trail starts inside a gate and follows red DEC disks under an impressive mixed growth forest of hemlock and yellow birch. At 0.3 mi. a side trail L leads to dark, conifer-ringed Black Pond. At 0.5 mi. the trail veers sharply L as a canoe carry goes straight ahead a short distance to Copperas Pond.

At 0.9 mi. another fork is reached as the trail goes R. To the L is a short canoe carry, leading to Whey Pond. A linear-shaped pond, Whey is noted locally for the quality of its brook trout fishing. The trail now begins to descend slightly and enters an expansive conifer swamp for a distance, crossing on wooden corduroy in two places, the last being the inlet to Little Square Pond, which lies off to the R at 2.2 mi.

The trail now rises as it ascends over the glacial ridges and knolls so prevalent in this area. A mature sugar maple, yellow birch, and hemlock forest gracefully arches over the trail. As it descends again a

DEC sign at 2.9 mi. points the way to a cross-over to the Floodwood Loop Trail (trail 13) on the other side of Fish Creek. Medium sized white birch trees denote intensive fires early in the century.

Floodwood Pond, one of the area's larger bodies of water, is seen off to the R in a number of spots for the next mile. At 4.5 mi. the trail reaches Rollins Pond Campsite beside campsite #256. This completes the link between the two large state campgrounds.

The trail now heads S following the vehicle access road joining the two campgrounds. For a distance it follows the shore of Rollins Pond, another one of the area's larger ponds. The extensive red pine plantation contrasts vividly with the native red pine stands on the eastern shores of some of the lakes traversed. Large white pine and white birch line the roadway.

The trail descends downhill where the far shores of Whey Pond are seen on the L at 6.6 mi. A gate at 7.1 mi. is generally considered the end of Rollins Pond Campground and the beginning of Fish Creek Ponds Campground. At 7.9 mi., go L at a Y intersection (R leads to NY 30). The trail continues to 8.4 mi., where the beginning of the loop is seen on the L. Square Pond with all of its many designated campsites is on the R. 1.1 mi. straight ahead is the trail's end in winter at the site of the caretaker's cabin.

Trail in Winter: *The trail in winter begins at the caretaker's cabin 100 yards inside the entrance. This is generally the limit of plowing and adds 1.1 mi. to the loop in both directions for a total distance of 10.6 mi. of cross-country skiing. The grade and width of the loop are generally well-suited to winter skiing with snowmobile activity only moderate.*

Distances: *Trailhead to Copperas Pond, 0.5 mi.; Whey Pond, 0.9 mi.; Little Square Pond, 2.2 mi.; Floodwood Loop Cross-over, 2.9 mi.; Rollins Pond campsite, 4.5 mi.; return to trailhead, 8.4 mi. (13.4 km). NOTE: In winter add 1.1 mi. in each direction. Ski trail starts at caretaker's cabin at edge of campground. Total distance: 10.6 mi. (17.0 km).*

Floodwood Road Section

Floodwood Rd. joins NY 30 9.4 mi. N of Wawbeek Corners, the intersection of NY 30 and NY 3. Wawbeek Corners is itself 6.0 mi. E of the village of Tupper Lake. Paved at the outset, Floodwood Rd. is a primarily gravel town road that, after passing some camps in the first half mile, proceeds 5.6 mi. through the Forest Preserve before dead-ending at the gates of a large private estate. It has a delightful network of trails clustered around it. Many of the trails link some of the glacial ponds that are so bounteous in this area. Others ascend moderate-sized peaks from which rich views of the entire area are had.

This section of the Adirondacks has an abundance of marked canoe carries linking many of the myriad bodies of water. These carries are usually short and all are marked by DEC yellow markers. The carries described are both representative of the other carries as a whole and in addition make appealing hikes on their own merits. This is due mostly to their moderate length (longer than most carries) and also to the beauty of the terrain traversed as they go about linking various bodies of water in the region. The first carry described is reached by a gravel town road; the latter two are accessible only by canoe.

Drainage is almost entirely through the west and middle branches of the St. Regis River. St. Regis also lends its name to the area's most imposing pinnacle which looms impressively over the conifer-clad, water-strewn lowland forests extending in all directions from its base. The St. Regis Canoe Area holds many of the trails here, with the remainder in the Saranac Lakes Wild Forest and on lands leased from Paul Smiths College.

This area is covered by the Upper Saranac Lake USGS topographic map, 7.5 x 15-min. series.

Short Hike:

Hoel Pond Trail – *1.6–mi. round-trip. This largely flat canoe carry leads to one of the many ponds of the St. Regis Canoe Area.*

Moderate Hike:

Floodwood Mt. Trail – *3.8–mi. round-trip. A walk on a woods road followed by a gradual climb that reveals the wonders of numerous wild, little-known mountains.*

Trail Described	Total Miles (one way)	Page
Hoel Pond Trail	0.8	66
Long Pond Trail/Canoe Carry	1.1	67
Rollins Pond Ski Trail	3.4	68
Floodwood Mt. Trail	1.9	69
Nellie Pond Trail/Canoe Carry	5.0	70
Long Pond Mt. Trail	1.4	71
Clamshell Pond Trail	3.8	73

(15) Hoel Pond Trail   Map: M-5

Trailhead: Access is from the Floodwood Rd. 1.0 mi. from its jct. with NY 30. The trail, marked with yellow disks by DEC as a canoe carry, starts at a small DEC sign on the R.

The trail, narrow and undulating, proceeds through a mostly mature forest of yellow birch, hemlock, and sugar maple for its first half. The presence of sugar maple indicates that the substrate over bedrock might be glacial till here, instead of the glacial outwash that is so common in this area.

At 0.7 mi. the trail meets and runs alongside a golf course for a short distance. Whiteface and Moose Mts. can be clearly seen looming impressively to the E. At 0.8 mi. the trail reaches Hoel Pond, with Long Pond Mt. towering above it on the far shore. Hoel Pond, actually an attractive, fairly large lake, is mostly in the Forest Preserve, with an area of private development on one shore.

Trail in winter: This trail is suitable for a relatively short cross-country ski route. Because the trail is narrow and curves sharply in places, caution should be exercised.

Distances: To Hoel Pond, 0.8 mi.; round-trip, 1.6 mi. (2.6 km).

(16) Long Pond Trail/Canoe Carry   Map: L-5

Trailhead: Access to this canoe carry is from Floodwood Rd. Take it W from NY 30 for 4.1 mi. to a DEC sign on the R just past the old Remsen–Lake Placid railroad track. This is the start of the trail.

The trail proceeds through a mature hemlock and yellow birch forest until a beaver pond is crossed on a corduroy at 0.4 mi. Some extra large white pine is also passed here. It continues in an undulating manner, passing a large creek at 0.6 mi. The trail continues under a mature forest to Long Pond at 1.1 mi.

Long Pond is the start of a canoe excursion winding up in Hoel Pond near the start of Floodwood Rd. Slang and Turtle ponds, utilizing only one short carry.

All of the Forest Preserve land N of the Floodwood Road and railroad tracks is designated as the St. Regis Canoe Area—unique so far in the Park. For the most part, this Canoe Area is administered as a Wilderness Area and motorboats are banned. The Forest Preserve land S of the Floodwood Rd. and E of the railroad tracks is in the Saranac Lakes Wild Forest.

Trail in winter: This trail is suited for cross-country skiing in winter. It provides a brief round trip or may be utilized as the first leg of an extended ski tour to Nellie Pond. See below.

Distance: Floodwood Road to Long Pond, 1.1 mi. (1.8 km).

(17) Rollins Pond Ski Trail

Map: K-5

Trailhead: Access is from an extension of Floodwood Rd. 0.8 mi. from where a caretaker's cabin R marks the former end of Forest Preserve lands. This point also marks the end of the town road. Recent state acquisition of the Floodwood Boy Scout Camp has extended the state boundary on the S side of the road. Access is from a rough parking area on the L unless the road is unplowed from the caretaker's cabin. In this case the ski trail begins here and proceeds along the road, increasing the distance 0.8 mi.

The trail, actually a private road, begins on the L by going through old fields in the process of being reforested after a severe fire. The boreal aspect of this region is reinforced by the balsam fir and black spruce reseeding directly here, in addition to the usual aspen, blueberries and spirea.

At 0.4 mi. the road crosses a creek on a bridge and proceeds uphill to a L turn at 1.0 mi. that leads to the Boy Scout Camp and the land they have retained in private ownership. The trail continues straight ahead through a forest of mainly second growth hardwoods.

At 1.4 mi. the lands reserved by the Boy Scouts end on the L. The road gradually becomes somewhat steeper as it undulates and crosses over several ridges. A number of creeks cross the trail, all draining into Floodwood and Rollins ponds as part of the Saranac River drainage. At 2.1 mi. a pond with extensive marshes on the L is the headwaters of Rollins Pond.

At 3.2 mi. the old Remsen-to-Lake Placid RR bed marks the end of Forest Preserve land. The last 0.2 mi. straight ahead has been retained by the Scouts. However, the Scouts are not in residence during the winter, so Rollins Pond can be reached easily then.

Trail in winter: *This trail's primary usage is as a cross-country ski route.*

Distances: *Floodwood Rd. extension parking area to fork, 1.0 mi.; to marshes, 2.1 mi.; to RR bed, 3.2 mi.; to Rollins Pond, 3.4 mi. (5.4 km).*

(18) Floodwood Mt. Trail   Map: K-5

This is a relatively moderate climb to the top of one of the area's minor peaks where on a clear day a mega-view can be had for a modest effort.

Trailhead: *Access is on the R at 1.1 mi. on the Rollins Pond Ski Trail, approximately 200 yds. past a L turn to the privately held Boy Scout Camp. At a low glacial boulder the trail, clearly marked by the red disks of the Floodwood Boy Scouts, takes off.*

The trail starts by gradually climbing through a second growth forest of white ash and maple. The tread of the path is quite clear in most places but in any event the red disks are clear all the way to the top. The trail runs along a babbling brook for a fair distance, crossing it in several places. The trail goes W upon reaching a shoulder of the mountain just under a point where a steep semi-cliff guides the last 0.2 mi. It turns sharply S for a distance and then goes W again before finally breaking out to the summit. An interesting feature in this hardwood forest is the size of some of the sugar maple and beech almost up to the crest of the peak. Trees do not diminish in size until just before the top, in marked contrast to most of the area's mountains. Slope exposure providing a favorable micro-climate probably accounts for this.

The view on top is superb, especially from October to May when the leaves are off the trees. There is a small open area on top but equal views are available just below the peak when the trees are leafless. Another viewpoint can be found past the summit, after a steep descent and ascent. St. Regis Mt. and Bay Pond Mt. to the N, Mt. Matumbla to the S, and Iron Mt. in the SW foreground all give a glimpse of how the area's peaks are arranged. Countless water bodies – relics of the glacier ice strewn below – including Rollins and Floodwood Pond, lie near its base. On an especially clear day the Seward Range can be seen in the southerly distance, remote and mysterious.

Trail in winter: *This trail is not suitable for cross-country skiing in winter due to steepness of terrain.*

Distances: *Floodwood Rd. extension to start of path marked with red disks, 1.1 mi.; to top of Floodwood Mt., 1.9 mi. (3.0 km).*

(19) Nellie Pond Trail/ Canoe Carry
Map: L-4

Trailhead: *The gravel road leading to the canoe put-in for access to this trail has been changed since publication of the last edition of this guide. The designated parking area is a newly constructed lot just off Floodwood Rd. to the R past the* railroad track. It is approximately 1.0 mi. W of the previous parking area on Floodwood Rd. and entails a longer canoe carry to the put-in for Long Pond.

The start of the trail is indicated by a DEC white wooden sign on the N shore of Long Pond. The trail, somewhat boggy in spots, proceeds on the level through a conifer swamp, passing a beaver pond on the L until it starts to ascend the shoulder of a beech and maple-crowned hill at 0.8 mi. It then descends and proceeds through another swamp, passing a side trail leading to Bessie Pond at 1.1 mi. At 1.4 mi. the shores of Nellie Pond are reached. Nellie, in addition to the usual conifers, is framed by a cliff on the E.

Trail in winter: *This trail becomes the final segment of an extended cross-country ski round-trip using the frozen waters of Long Pond as a pivot. Ski 1.1 mi. down the Long Pond Trail (trail 16) to the S shore of Long Pond. Ski due E on Long Pond until the lake veers sharply to the N in 0.5 mi. Now ski directly N for approximately 2.0 mi. into a large bay on the far shore. A white wooden sign here indicates the start of the trail to Nellie Pond. Several steep pitches are encountered on the ski to Nellie Pond.*

Distances: *Summer: Long Pond to Nellie Pond, 1.4 mi. (2.3 km). Winter: Floodwood Rd. to Long Pond, 1.1 mi.; Long Pond to North Bay at start of Nellie Pond Trail, 3.6 mi.; to Nellie Pond, 5.0 mi.; round-trip, 10.0 mi. (16.0 km).*

Long Pond Mt. Trail

Map: L-4

Trailhead: *This is a bushwhack reached only by canoe on Long Pond after a 0.3 mi. carry from the parking lot on Floodwood Rd. The parking lot itself is 5.4 mi. from NY 30 on the S side of Floodwood Rd. Proceed due E on Long Pond for 2.0 mi. until the Lake turns N. It is 1.5 mi. of further paddling to a bay on the far N shore where there may be a sign for the canoe carry to Mountain Pond. Begin hiking here.*

The trail ascends fairly steeply through a conifer plantation to crest on a summit and then descends to the shores of Mountain Pond at 0.6 mi. This is the end of the visible path.

Follow a faint path made by fishermen to the R as it encircles the pond and arrives on the far side approximately opposite a point across from the end of the visible path. Take a compass reading of 360 (due N) and begin the climb, which is gradual at first, then becomes quite steep in several sections, through a mixed northern hardwood-hemlock forest with occasional large specimens of hardwoods rising above the general canopy. Rock outcrops and cliffs have to be skirted in a number of places. The route generally parallels a hemlock ravine for a distance before levelling off briefly at a false summit. At 0.8 mi. the level, grassy summit is finally reached.

The view on top can be outstanding on a clear day. Mt. Matumbla is clearly etched to the SW while the sprawling forests to the N lead up to St. Regis Mt. towering above the lowland forests. Many of the lakes of the St. Regis Canoe Area are clearly visible, as are the towers of Tupper Lake to the SW. On a really good day Whiteface Mt. can be seen in the distance, clearly defined by its rock slides and the cirque up high near the summit. Adding to the charm of the trip is the pleasing spectacle of pink corydalis in bloom among crevices in the cliffs just under the summit.

Trail in winter: *Except for the 3.5 mi. on the surface of Long Pond when frozen, the trail is generally not suitable for cross-country skiing in winter. Steepness and lack of a marked trail are the main impediments here.*

Distances: *To Mountain Pond, 0.6 mi.; to summit of Long Pond Mountain, 1.4 mi. (2.2 km).*

(21) Clamshell Pond Trail

Trailhead: *Take the first R turn on Floodwood Rd. at 0.3 mi. and proceed along a golf course to arrive at the edge of the woods. Turn L and drive 0.1 mi. down the gravel road to a parking area by the canoe put-in. (In winter, it is necessary to park carefully by the turn and ski or snowshoe the 0.1 mi. to the put-in.) Paddle NW approximately 1.5 mi. to a RR bed. Carry over to the RR bed to Turtle Pond. An approximate 0.1 mi. paddle NW leads to the start of the trail marked with small DEC signs on the shore.*

The beginning of the trail is indicated by a white wooden marker on the shore of Turtle Pond. White pines line the long and narrow pond here. At 0.1 mi. the trail passes a Norway spruce plantation, incongruous in this otherwise natural setting. At 0.3 mi. large native red spruce are encountered as a swamp is crossed on a corduroy. A large beaver vlei is seen to the L. The trail then ascends a hill crowned with mature birch and sugar maple at 0.5 mi. before starting a descent to reach the conifer-rimmed shores of Clamshell Pond in 1.3 mi. An abundance of freshwater mussels gave this pond its name.

Trail in winter: *The trail may be used as the last segment of an extended cross-country round trip. Ski the 1.5 mi. NW across Hoel Pond to the RR. Cross over the tracks and continue skiing NW for 1.0 mi. to the far shore at a point where a DEC wooden sign points the way to Clamshell Pond. Ski the 1.3 mi. to Clamshell Pond. The ascent and descent of the hill toward Turtle Pond are quite steep and caution should be exercised.*

Distances: *Summer: Turtle Pond to Clamshell Pond, 1.3 mi. (2.0 km). Winter: Start of trail to RR grade separating Hoel Pond from Turtle Pond, 1.5 mi.; Turtle Pond to start of final segment to Clamshell Pond, 2.5 mi.; Clamshell Pond, 3.8 mi.; round trip, 7.6 mi. (12.2 km).*

Paul Smiths Section

Paul Smiths College, noted for its school of forestry and hotel management, is the site of the Adirondack Park Visitor Interpretive Center and an attractive nature trail on the grounds of the college. In addition, there is a small series of trails in the St. Regis Canoe Area surrounding the college. These trails link the area's glacial ponds and ascend the peak of a modest but dramatic mountain. The isolated Azure Mt. trail is also placed here. For Everton Falls Trail, see p. 231. Several of the trails in the first edition have been deleted from the second edition for a variety of reasons including abandonment, flooding, indistinctness or inaccessibility of trailhead. The area is covered by the following USGS topographic maps: St. Regis Mt. 7.5 x 15 min. series and Meno 7.5-min. series.

Short Hike:

Azure Mt. Trail – *2.0-mi. round trip. A short but steep ascent leads to an open summit with marvelous long-distance views in three directions.*

Moderate Hike:

Fish Pond Truck Trail – *10.2-mi. round trip. This nearly level route is intersected by several canoe carries leading to the shores of ponds in the St. Regis Canoe Area.*

Harder Hike:

St. Regis Mt. – *5.0-mi. round trip. A strenuous climb is rewarded with superb panoramas of peaks and ponds.*

(22) Fish Pond Truck Trail   Map: M-4

This is a former state truck trail now barred to vehicular traffic in conformity with the State Land Master Plan. The unmarked DEC trail, mainly undulating with one moderately steep section, goes through the heart of the St. Regis Canoe Area to a wild, remote lake fashioned by the last retreating glacier. The St. Regis Canoe Area itself embraces over 18,000 acres and is essentially managed as a Wilderness Area.

Trailhead: *Access is from the Fish Hatchery Rd., a short loop road that leaves NY 30 11.3 mi. N of its intersection with NY 3 at Wawbeek Corners. A marked DEC trailhead is on the L here. Turn L off the loop road, then L again at the abandoned RR crossing. Proceed about 0.5 mi. past the numbered campsites to a R turn; the Truck Trail gate is just ahead to the L of the parking lot.*

The trail begins by passing through an area of mature yellow birch with young conifers coming in underneath. At 1.0 mi large white pine is encountered, followed by a beaver pond crossed just above the dam at 1.3 mi. Beaver activity is common along this trail, but since most of the crossings are over culverts of the former DEC truck route, flooding is not usually a problem. At 1.6 mi. the trail passes through a spruce-cedar swamp and shortly thereafter begins to ascend, reaching a height at 2.0 mi.

At 2.2 mi. a large grey bedrock outcrop is seen on the L. The trail now makes a gradual descent to the first of the many side trails serving primarily as canoe carries to some of the ancillary ponds of the area at 2.6 mi. on the R. This is the carry to St. Regis Pond. At 2.8 mi. another trail comes in on the L. This is the carry to Grassy Pond. At 3.2 mi. the canoe carry to Ochre Pond comes in on the R. These three relatively short canoe carry trails are described below (trails 22A, 22B, 22C).

The trail continues ahead until at 3.5 mi. it begins to descend more steeply from the ridge it has been travelling. Large specimens of sugar maple are now seen for the first time on the well-drained soil of the ridge. At 3.8 mi. two large gravel pits on the L provided the material for the truck trail. This truck trail was originally paved, at least rudimentarily, and remnants of some paving stones can occasionally be noted.

At 4.8 mi. a ridge is seen on the R. Directly behind the ridge lies the enchanting Mud Pond – from which another canoe carry trail also leads to Fish Pond.

At 5.1 mi. the trail reaches Fish Pond. With several excellent campsites nearby, Fish Pond is set amidst gorgeous surroundings. There are two lean-tos on the shores of Fish Pond – one to the L of the trail and the other across the lake on the far shore. There is a beaver dam R at the inlet of the bay on which the trail terminates. All around this shore are large specimens of hemlock, while on the far shore white pine line the pond.

Trail in winter: *Admirably suited as a cross-country ski trail, it receives heavy use as such in winter. The way is wide and usually well cleared, with a steep, twisting* *ascent and descents toward the middle.*

Distances: *Gate to St. Regis Pond Carry, 2.6 mi.; to Grassy Pond Carry, 2.8 mi.; to Ochre Pond Carry, 3.2 mi.; to Fish Pond, 5.1 mi. (8.2 km).*

Canoe Carries

The following canoe carries all begin on the Fish Pond Truck Trail (see above). They proceed through majestic stands of trees to reach remote, jewel-like bodies of water lying in magnificent scenic settings.

(22A) St. Regis Pond Canoe Carry Map: M-4

Trailhead: *This short but worthwhile canoe carry trail starts at mile 2.6 of the Fish Pond Truck Trail (see above).*

The trail leads through a mixed forest to a quiet bay of St. Regis Pond, which is rimmed mostly by mature spruce and pine. A DEC fish barrier dam is across the outlet at the point where it flows out of this bay. Above this dam the native brook trout has its main habitat, and the dam's primary function is to prevent non-native, so-called "warm water" fish from entering the trout waters and probably outcompeting the native fish.

Trail in winter: *Suited for a brief ski trip.*

Distance: *Truck trail to St. Regis Pond: 0.2 mi. (0.3 km).*

(22B) Grassy Pond Canoe Carry   Map: M-4

Trailhead: This trail begins as a side trail coming into the Fish Pond Truck Trail (see above) on the L at 2.8 mi.

The trail proceeds through a hardwood forest with a heavy undergrowth of hobblebush lining both sides of the trail. It descends slightly to arrive on the shores of Grassy Pond at 0.5 mi. Large white pines are on the shore and a rim of sedges encircles the pond. A large spruce swamp is visible at the S end.

Trail in winter: Suited for a brief ski trip.

Distance: Truck trail to Grassy Pond: 0.5 mi. (0.8 km).

(22C) Ochre Pond Canoe Carry   Map: M-4

Trailhead: This carry trail begins on a side trail intersecting the Fish Pond Truck Trail (see above) on the R at 3.2 mi.

The trail starts with monarch specimens of white pine on its R. At 0.2 mi. a large yellow birch on the R. has its roots completely enveloping a glacial boulder. This situation probably originated when a seed of a yellow birch germinated on the inviting moss that lay atop the boulder some 75 or more years ago. At 0.3 mi. Ochre Pond itself, rimmed with large white pine, is framed by the twin specter of St. Regis Mt. and Little St. Regis Mt. looming above it.

Trail in winter: Suited for a brief ski trip.

Distance: Truck trail to Ochre Pond, 0.3 mi. (0.5 km).

(23) Red Dot Trail

No Map

Trailhead: Access is from the Church Pond Rd., a gravel road going N from NY 192, 0.1 mi. E of its junction with NY 30. Yellow disks and a register are on the R 100 yds. down the road.

This loop has been marked as a nature trail by Paul Smiths College and attractive wooden plaques line the route identifying features of the local flora and fauna. The land which the trail traverses is currently in the process of being transferred from Paul Smiths to NY State, mainly as a conservation easement.

The trail is marked with yellow as it enters the forest and proceeds as a spur to the red-marked loop. At 0.3 mi. a junction is reached just past an old log road. A R turn here leads in 100 yds. to an imposing group of white pines clustered together and known locally as "Cathedral Pines." A sign should indicate this.

The trail reaches straight to another junction at 0.5 mi. This is the actual Red Dot Loop – veer R here for now; the L trail is the return. At 0.7 mi. the trail reaches a lean-to on the shores of Church Pond. The forest here is an impressive one of white and red pine along with hemlock and white birch, with many mature trees in evidence.

The trail goes over a canal between Church and Little Osgood Pond on a small wooden bridge at 0.8 mi. and continues along the canal between Little Osgood and Osgood Pond, passing the return leg at 0.9 mi. The canal, locally called Paul Smiths Canal, was constructed early in the century to link the water of Osgood Pond with the St. Regis lakes. At 1.0 mi. it comes to the shores of Osgood Pond and ends at 1.1 mi. at the site of a boat ramp on Osgood Pond, a large, sprawling lake that stands in sharp contrast to the two small kettle ponds first reached by the loop.

Return 0.2 mi. to a point where a bridge goes over the canal on the R. The trail crosses the bridge and proceeds to a lean-to on the shores of Little Osgood Pond at 1.4 mi. It continues on an esker overlooking Osgood Pond to the original loop junction at 1.8 mi. A R here leads back to the trailhead at 2.3 mi.

Trail in Winter: *Suited for skiing in winter, used by students of college.*

Distances: *Church Pond Rd. to lean-to on Church Pond, 0.7 mi.; to Osgood Pond, 1.0 mi.; to lean-to on Little Osgood Pond, 1.4 mi.; to beginning, 2.3 mi. (3.7 km).*

(24) St. Regis Mt. Trail   Map: M-3

This DEC red-marked trail makes a relatively short, steep climb to the summit of an isolated northern Adirondack peak with magnificent views in nearly all directions. A closed fire tower dominates the top.

Trailhead: *Access is from NY 30 7.3 mi. N of Lake Clear Jct. Turn L on Keese Mills Rd. here, passing Paul Smiths College on the L, and proceed W approximately 2.4 mi. to where a gravel road comes in on the L. Take this gravel road approximately 0.6 mi. to the trailhead parking lot on the R just before a gate. Inside the gate is Topridge, the former estate of Marjorie Merriweather Post.*

The trail starts by gradually rising in terrain that undulates rather sharply. The first portion of the trail is on Paul Smiths College land and passes through large specimens of sugar maple and birch with occasional glacial erratics of anorthosite. At 0.6 mi. the trail passes the out-buildings of Camp Topridge on the L and at 0.8 mi. encounters the telephone line that formerly served the fire tower on the summit. At 1.5 mi. the ranger cabin is noted on the L, and shortly thereafter the trail begins to rise steeply using water bars constructed by Paul Smiths forestry students in places. At 2.0 mi. the trail levels off somewhat among large specimens of white birch.

At 2.2 mi. the trail follows a sign to the R. Disregard the old eroded trail going straight ahead. Striped maple, beloved of deer and moose, now begins to appear in the understory.

At 2.3 mi. the trail goes L at another fork and rises sharply to attain the mostly bare summit at 2.5 mi. The bareness of the summit and the presence of white birch attest to the surveyors under Verplanck Colvin. A few stunted spruce and fir are as usual present on the top, along with mountain ash.

The High Peaks along with Mt. McKenzie and the Seward Range can be seen to the S. Directly below, a multitude of ponds nestling in the St. Regis Canoe Area can also readily be seen. Slightly to the NE the isolated peaks of DeBar and Loon Lake mts. stand out clearly.

Trail in Winter: Unsuitable due to steepness of terrain.

Distance: Topridge gate to fire tower, 2.5 mi. (4.0 km).

(25) Azure Mt. Trail
Page Map

This is another short, steep climb to one of the isolated northern Adirondack peaks that usually stand in a sea of green forest.

Trailhead: Access to this DEC red-marked trail is from the Blue Mountain Rd., which goes S from NY 458 approximately 4.0 mi. S of St. Regis Falls and 3 mi. N of the hamlet of Santa Clara. Proceed approximately 7.0 mi. S until a dirt road comes in on the R. It is 0.1 mi. down the dirt road to a gate, room to park a few cars, and the start of the trail.

The trail begins at the gate and starts out fairly level, reaching an abandoned fire observer's cabin and other outbuildings at 0.3 mi. The trail markers continue between the outbuildings. The trail begins to rise immediately, passing through a pole-sized maple grove with

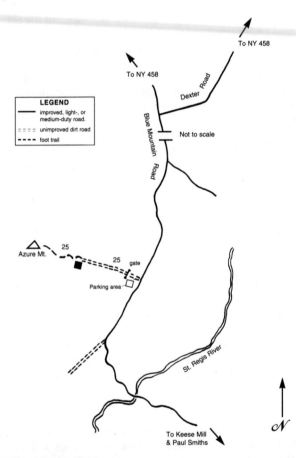

Azure Mountain Trail (25)
Based on Meno quadrangle

occasional white ash. At 0.5 mi. both white and yellow birch begin to appear. This usually indicates a past burn.

The trail now starts to weave in and out of an eroded herd path that proceeds straight up the slope of the mountain at a perpendicular axis to the fall line. The trail crisscrosses the old herd path for the rest of the steep pitch and eventually reaches the crest of the hill at 0.9 mi., with the open summit slightly beyond at 1.0 mi. The summit is dominated by an old fire tower, still standing but not manned and not recommended for climbing. The summit in early October is festooned with pin cherry and chokecherry in fruit and also laced with trails through the shrubbery made by bears in quest of the fruit. Whiteface, Marcy and the Sewards are clearly seen to the S; DeBar Mt. looms large to the E, while below lie some of the shimmering ponds of the St. Regis Canoe Area. To the N. the farm lands and settlements of the St. Lawrence Valley can be discerned.

Trail in winter: unsuitable for cross-country skiing.

Distance: Blue Mountain Rd. to summit of Azure Mt., 1.0 mi. (1.6 km).

Visitor Interpretive Center

The Adirondack Park Visitor Interpretive Center, which portrays and interprets the many facets of the Adirondack Park, was opened at Paul Smiths in 1988. A smaller center was subsequently opened in Newcomb in the central Adirondacks. The Visitor Center at Paul Smiths is located off NY 30 approximately 0.2 mi. N of Paul Smiths College.

The center, under the supervision of the Adirondack Park Agency, is located in a handsome, spacious building erected as a replica of one of the traditional "Great Camps" for which the Adirondacks were renowned. A full spectrum of historical and ecological displays pertinent to the Adirondacks is featured at the center, which is open year-round.

An interconnecting network of short interpretive trails emanates from the main building to make various loops through the scenic glacial topography that abounds at the center. With slight variations these trails are converted to excellent cross-country ski routes in winter. A listing of the trails with a brief synopsis of their outstanding features is found below. Further information may be had from maps and materials at the Visitor Center itself.

Trails

The following trails are reached from the same area in back of the main building. Generally, one begins where another ends.

a) Heron Marsh Trail – 0.8 mi. (1.3 k m)

Begins the network of trails. Boardwalk from side of trail provide vistas of an expansive freshwater marsh with Jenkins Mt. in the background. Large white pine with sheep laurel below line the way.

b) Shingle Mill Falls Trail – 0.6 mi. (1.0 km)

Trail starts where #1 ends. Total –1.1 mi. from main building. A bridge goes directly over marsh, and an enchanting natural waterfall is passed along the way.

c) Forest Ecology Trail – 1.2 mi. (1.9 km)

This trail 2.2 mi. from building, also crosses marsh on bridge, and starts at a point on Shingle Mill Falls Trail. The marsh is a natural wetland whose size was increased by a dam erected mainly for wildlife purposes by Paul Smiths College. Trail goes through a variety of forest habitats.

d) Silviculture Trail – 1.0 mi. (1.6 km)

Reached from a point on Forest Ecology Trail. Total length 3.5 mi. from building. Details and illustrates various forestry systems and methods of harvesting trees along its route. Can also be reached from the Keese Mills Road.

e) Barnum Brook Trail – 0.6 mi. (1.0 km)

Reached from side of building. Crosses rustic bridges over a rushing brook with views of St. Regis Mt. in background. Bridges and trails were constructed by prisoners at a nearby correctional facility under the direction of DEC. This trail is reserved for snowshoers in winter.

Cross-Country Ski Trails

These ski routes result from a combination of the above interpretive trails plus an unplowed gravel road that leads to Jenkins Mt. The trails, which are coded in different colors, are generally easy to moderate in difficulty with only a few fairly steep downhill sections.

a) Esker Ski Trail – 4.5 mi. (7.2 km)

Color code green. The longest ski loop. Utilizes Heron Marsh, Shingle Mill Falls and Silviculture trails, plus the unplowed Jenkins Mt. Rd. in making a loop to and from the building.

b) Tamarack Ski Trail – 2.8 mi. (4.5 km)

Color code orange. An abbreviated version of the above loop. Leaves Esker Ski Trail at a spur across bog walkway to ski downslope to Jenkins Mt. Rd. and return to building.

c) Heron Marsh Loop Ski Trail – 1.5 mi. (2.4 km)

Color coded blue-purple. The shortest of the ski loops, this one uses the Esker Ski Trail to branch off and make a brief circuit via the dam at Shingle Falls Mill.

DeBar Wild Forest Section

The sprawling DeBar Wild Forest, which stretches from just N of Paul Smiths to the boundary of the Adirondack Park, is framed in its main section by the twin pinnacles of DeBar and Baldface Mountain. Trails to the summit of these wild and aloof peaks – one marked, one a bushwhack – are prominent features of the hikes in this section.

From the base of these two sentinels an almost uninterrupted boreal forest unfurls in all directions as far as the eye can register. Bogs and swamps are common, ponds and lakes less so, especially in contrast to the St. Regis Canoe Area and Saranac Lake Wild Forest to the S. There are some, however, and several of the trails have them as their destination. Meandering streams and pine-clad eskers are also a prominent feature of the terrain traversed by the trails. The outlying Lyon Mt. Trail is placed in this grouping for purposes of convenience and clarity. For Everton Falls Trail, see p. 231.

The Tent Platform Trail described in the first edition has been dropped, as has the Campsite Trail. The obscurity of the trail over East Mt. has progressed to the point that it has also been deleted from this edition.

A DEC campsite is located at Meacham Lake. This area is covered by the following USGS topographic maps: Meacham Lake 7.5 min. series and DeBar Mt. 7.5 min. series.

Moderate Hike:

Hayes Brook Truck Trail – *7.2–mi. round trip. An easy walk ends in a charming clearing surrounded by mountains.*

Harder Hike:

Lyon Mt. – *5.0–mi. round trip. A steady climb is rewarded with views ranging from the skyscrapers of Montreal to the high peaks of Vermont and the Adirondacks.*

Trail Described	Total Miles (one way)	Page
Hayes Brook Truck Trail	3.6	88
Grassy Pond Trail	1.4	91
Slush Pond Ski Trail	2.5	92
Kettle Trail	3.2	92
DeBar Game Mgmt. Area Trail	7.7	94
Beaver Valley Trail	0.7	98
DeBar Mt. Trail	2.6	99
DeBar Pond Trail	0.3	101
Lyon Mt. Trail	2.5	101

(26) Hayes Brook Truck Trail   Page Map

This DEC yellow-marked trail, mostly following the route of an old DEC truck trail, proceeds to an old meadow deep in the DeBar Wild Forest where several lean-tos and horse shelters are located. The trail has been marked at various times in the past as both a horse trail and a snowmobile trail.

Trailhead: *Access is from NY 30 approximately 10.7 mi. N of Lake Clear Jct. (NY 30 and NY 86) and 3.7 mi. N of Paul Smiths College. A DEC sign at a gravel road is on the R. Take this road 0.2 mi. to the trailhead on the L at a gated truck trail.*

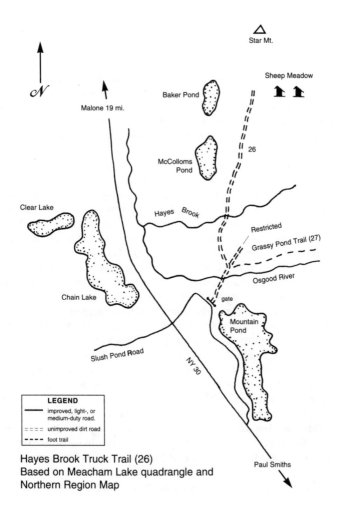

Hayes Brook Truck Trail (26)
Based on Meacham Lake quadrangle and
Northern Region Map

The trail starts around the metal gate following the old truck trail through a pine plantation. (The yellow snowmobile and horse trail markers follow a cut trail through the pines that rejoins the main trail at 0.3 mi.) At 0.5 mi. the trail crosses the Osgood River on a wooden bridge. Tamarack and white pine line its banks here. Shortly after, the marked trail turns sharply L and makes a sharp ascent in a pine plantation. The truck trail continues straight ahead to rejoin the hiking trail at 1.5 mi. The Grassy Pond Trail (see below) begins 50 ft. ahead on R off the truck trail.

The trail, after leaving the truck trail, begins a sharply undulating course through a mature red pine plantation with a luxurious undergrowth of bracken fern. This course continues until the truck trail is rejoined at 1.5 mi. The trail turns L here and crosses Hayes Brook on a wooden bridge. The brook is choked with alders in this particular spot. Farther upstream, the headwaters of Hayes Brook are an important winter deer yard for this whole area.

At 1.8 mi. the trail levels off and passes a flat sandy area with large white pine and an understory of balsam and spruce. These are the boreal sand flats which are quite common elsewhere in this section. At 2.8 mi. old meadows on the R have conifers directly reforesting them. This happens quite often in this section due to the prevalence of conifers as a source of seed stock.

An old trail comes in at 3.4 mi. A DEC sign here states that the trail is not maintained and is difficult to follow. It can be followed easily for a relatively short distance until blowdowns and wet areas start to impede progress. The trail would eventually reach the DeBar Game Management Area and ultimately Meacham Lake, but the way is additionally barred by posted private land that protrudes into the DeBar Wild Forest. It is therefore probably better to consider this route as a round trip type of bushwhack (which it is in places, given the obscurity of the trail) than as a regular marked trail. It does, however, provide a trek through some interesting boreal habitat and ultimately ascends the shoulder of East Mt.

At 3.6 mi. the old Sheep Meadow is finally reached. Two DEC lean-tos and shelters for horses are located here. The old clearing, where sheep were formerly pastured, presents a charming setting, being entirely encircled by mountains.

Trail in winter: *Suitable for cross-country skiing.*

Distances: *Gate to Osgood River, 0.5 mi.; to Hayes Brook, 1.5 mi.; to old Sheep Meadow and lean-tos, 3.6 mi. (5.8 km).*

(27) Grassy Pond Trail   Map: N-1

Trailhead: *The unmarked Grassy Pond Trail starts at 0.6 mi. of the Hayes Brook Truck Trail (see above). It leads through some stunning boreal habitat at the edge of the Forest Preserve on Grassy Pond.*

The trail starts by following an old jeep trail passing between towering white pine on an esker on the L and the valley on the Osgood River on the R. It begins a slow descent into a spruce and tamarack swamp at 1.0 mi. and continues through the swamp until Grassy Pond is seen on the L at 1.4 mi. Grassy Pond is semi-circular and mostly lives up to its name – it is almost completely encircled by a mat of grass-like sedges with some cattails in places. Owing to a recent state acquisition, the entire pond, including the old lean-to on the far shore, is now Forest Preserve.

Trail in Winter: *Suitable for cross-country skiing.*

Distance: *Hayes Brook Truck Trail to Grassy Pond, 1.4 mi. (2.2 km).*

(28) Slush Pond Ski Trail

This generally unplowed gravel road leads for 2.5 mi. through Forest Preserve to the gate of a large private park. It is marked part-way as a snowmobile trail and receives moderate cross-country ski use in winter.

Trailhead: *Access is from the gravel road opposite the Hayes Brook Truck Trail (trail 26) 3.7 mi. N of Paul Smiths on NY 30.*

The trail is mostly level as it proceeds through an extensive evergreen plantation to reach Slush Pond on the R at 2.0 mi. Slush Pond is typical of many boreal bodies of water in this area – entirely ringed by conifers and marsh. The monolithic pine plantations here were an attempt at reforestation after the disastrous forest fires early in the century almost completely denuded many entire sections of woodland. Several primitive campsites are located on the L under the pines. The road and trail ends at the gate of the private estate at 2.5 mi.

Trail in Winter: *This trail's primary usage is as a cross-country ski trail.*

Distances: *NY 30 to Slush Pond and campsites 2.0 mi.; end of trail, 2.5 mi. (4.0 km)*

(29) Kettle Trail

Trailhead: *The start of this trail is at 0.6 mi. on the Slush Pond Rd. (trail). Begin on the R following the red snowmobile disks attached so prominently to the pine trees.*

The trails starts on the R by entering an extensive plantation of

Scotch and red pine which follow the trail almost the entire route. The deep shade and consequent lack of sunlight under the pines has severely limited the undergrowth although, in places, maple and balsam fir saplings can be observed trying to subsist along with the ever-present bracken fern.

The trail is on an esker at the beginning and then takes an undulating course over several kame-like hills. Further evidence of glacial topography is encountered in the presence of a number of kettle holes along the way. These legacies of the glacial ice are especially interesting as they are here seen in all stages of succession from the original ponds that existed after the ice melted.

At 3.0 mi. the trail reaches the first kettle pond off to the R – it still exists as a pond, albeit a very shallow one. At 0.6 mi. another kettle is passed on the R. The pond here has progressed to a bog – as the waving plumes of cotton grass growing on the quaking sphagnum mat attest so elegantly.

The next two kettles have almost achieved the ultimate in progression; they are now completely dry land. However, because they lie in a frost bracket and have a high water table after snow melt in the spring, they have not been reforested as all other dry areas in this region have been. Instead, their bottoms are covered with a thick growth of spirea and blueberry, which play a part in retarding tree growth.

The last kettle pond is a field just before the trail makes a L zig zag turn around private land at 2.2 mi. The trail proceeds another mile to dead-end at a gravel road at 3.2 mi.; this point is generally considered the end of the trail. A R on the gravel road (which may be driven with care during summer) leads to NY 30 in 1.9 mi. Another 2.4 mi. S on NY 30 leads to the start of the Slush Pond Road, from where the trail begins.

Trail in winter: *This trail is generally well-adapted to cross-country skiing in* *winter. Add 1.2 mi. to total round trip as Slush Pond Rd. is usually unplowed.*

Distances: *Slush Pond Rd. to first kettle pond, 0.3 mi.; to second kettle pond, 0.6 mi.; to last pond, 2.2 mi.; to gravel road, 3.2 mi. (5.1 km).*

(30) DeBar Game Management Area Trail

Page Map

This lengthy trail, only sporadically marked with both red and yellow disks, starts at the gravel pit in the Meacham Lake campsite and proceeds through the heart of the old DeBar Game Management Area to a gravel road off NY 99. This area, unique in the Forest Preserve, was once the scene of an initially successful attempt to return elk to the Adirondacks. The elk, the gift of the governor of a western state to the governor of New York, were originally held in pens here before being gradually released to spread through the northern Adirondacks. The elk persisted from the 1930s until approximately 1960 when they finally disappeared—mostly due to poaching. The Game Management Area itself was set up for agricultural and wildlife propagation purposes and was not to be in the Forest Preserve.

Trailhead: *Access is from the DEC campsite at Meacham Lake, at 1,203 acres the second largest lake whose borders are entirely in the Forest Preserve. Relatively unaffected by acid rain, it has an excellent fishery of lake trout and northern pike with at least one endangered species, the whitefish, present in some numbers. Campsite access is off NY 30 9.5 mi. N of Paul Smiths. A DEC campsite road comes in on the R here. Take this road to the entrance to the campsite. There is a slight fee for day use.*

From this point it is 0.5 mi. to the start of the DeBar Game Management Area Trail, and also the DeBar Mt. Trail which begins along the Game Management Trail. A dirt road leads W at campsite 48 to the trail's beginning at the site of an old gravel pit. Vehicles may be parked here. The gate banning vehicle access is to the R.

To make possible a one-way hike, a second car can be parked at the N end of the trail. To reach this point, return to NY 30 and proceed N 8.2 mi. to the intersection with NY 99. Turn R on NY 99 and go 8.9 mi. to a gravel road on the R. It is 1.3 mi. on this road to the trailhead.

The trail begins by rising slightly in a mixed forest with occasional large yellow birch. At 0.3 mi. the trail stays R at an intersection. The trail so far is marked sporadically with DEC markers of both red and yellow. At 0.5 mi. a large, mostly open spruce bog is passed on the L. The typical bog vegetation is prominent here—leatherleaf, cotton-grass, etc.

At 0.7 mi. the trail begins to pass through a spruce flat with scattered fir. The outlet to Winnebago Pond is crossed at 1.0 mi. Winnebago Pond is another small northern Adirondack kettle pond that is in the process of reverting to a bog. At 1.1 mi. another trail intersection is reached – to the L the red trail markers denote the start of the DeBar Mt. Trail (trail 31).

The trail continues R from the intersection and passes an old beaver flow on the L at 1.6 mi. Shortly thereafter, at 1.8 mi. it enters the DeBar Wildlife Management Area. A little distance ahead, yellow horse trail signs in several places were probably placed here to avoid excessively wet areas along the trail.

At 2.1 mi. the trail crosses a creek on a wooden bridge and passes through a mixed forest in beginning to rise somewhat for the first time. At 2.6 mi. a sign on the R saying "trail not maintained" is encountered. Disregard this sign – it alludes to a side trail now officially abandoned – and continue on an old tote road to a fork at 3.1 mi. where a fork in the road is encountered.

The trail continues L, rising moderately, crossing another

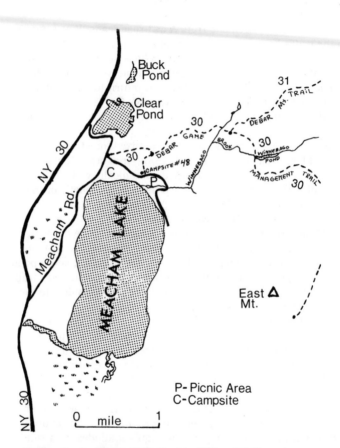

Buck Pond

Clear Pond

Buck Pond

31

DEBAR MT. TRAIL

30

30

DEBAR GAME

WINNEBAGO BROOK

WINNEBAGO POND

30

CAMPSITE #48

30

MANAGEMENT TRAIL

30

NY 30

Meacham Rd.

C

P

MEACHAM LAKE

East Mt. △

P- Picnic Area
C- Campsite

NY 30

0   mile   1

DeBar Game Mgmt. (30), Beaver Valley (30A), and
DeBar Mt. (31) trails
Based on Meacham Lake and DeBar Mt. quadrangles

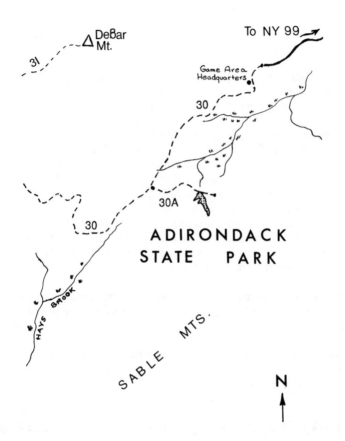

To NY 99

DeBar Mt.

31

Game Area Headquarters

30

30A

ADIRONDACK
STATE   PARK

HAYS BROOK

30

SABLE MTS.

N

wooden bridge at 3.2 mi. At 3.4 mi. it begins to cross through a swamp using a corduroy bridge. The trail rises again through a hardwood forest with only an occasional sign present, to another intersection of two old tote roads. The trail goes L and continues through a mixed forest, crossing several creeks until another old trail goes R at 4.6 mi. This is the start of the trail to Beaver Valley (trail 30A).

The trail passes one of the wildlife ponds constructed in the days of the Game Management Area at 5.1 mi. At 5.2 mi. a semi-cleared area marks the site of a former DEC education camp. The trail passes still another side trail at 5.9 mi. This is one of the tote roads constructed during Game Management days to branch off and reconnect with the main tote road.

At 6.0 mi. the trail passes some wetlands drained by Hatch Brook on the R and shortly after passes another spur to the R that leads to more of the area's man-made ponds. These ponds are quite novel for the Forest Preserve.

Trail in winter: This trail is admirably suited as a cross-country ski trail. Add 1.3 mi. to take trail to Country Route 99 where another car may be parked. Total distance in winter: 9.0 mi.

Distances: Gated truck trail and gravel pit in Meacham Lake Campsite to start of DeBar Mt. Trail, 1.1 mi.; to start of Beaver Valley Trail, 4.6 mi.; to boundary of old refuge and end of trail, 7.7 mi. (12.3 km).

(30A) Beaver Valley Trail   Page Map

Trailhead: An unmarked trail to Beaver Valley starts on the R at 4.6 mi. on the DeBar Game Management Trail (see above).

This trail gives access to a pretty man-made pond constructed during the wildlife management era in this area. The trail goes through some hardwoods and a medium-sized conifer plantation before arriving at the pond in Beaver Valley at 0.7 mi. While the artificial dam and spillway are readily apparent here, the scene today is both secluded and blissful—framed on two sides by protective hills looming above it.

Trail in Winter: *Suitable for a short side excursion from Game Management Trail in winter.*

Distance: *DeBar Game Management Trail to Beaver Valley Pond, 0.7 mi. (1.1 km).*

(31) DeBar Mt. Trail Page Map

The red-marked trail to the top of Debar Mt. starts on the DeBar Game Management Trail (see above) and ascends the massive hulk of one of the most prominent isolated peaks in the northern Adirondacks. The peak, in a remote setting, looms large on the horizon from all directions. The view on top, while worthwhile, does not quite live up to the promise DeBar gives from the valley floor.

This peak, like many, was scorched by fire early this century. The dryness of these peaks, their thin soil and attractiveness to lightning, combined with their inaccessibility to firefighting apparatus, make them extremely vulnerable to fire.

Trailhead: *The trail begins at 1.1 mi. on the DeBar Game Management Trail. The sporadically red-marked trail to the L is the DeBar Mt. Trail; the R fork is the continuation of the Game Management trails.*

The trail is mostly flat at the start, beginning to rise moderately at 0.3 mi. under a canopy of large yellow birch. It continues rising moderately as sugar maple and beech begin to replace the yellow birch.

At 0.9 mi. the trail begins to level off and crosses a shoulder between two peaks—Baldface L with DeBar on the R. At 1.8 mi. a DEC lean-to is seen on the L. Just beyond is a small meadow with the foundation of the fire observer's old cabin still noticeable. The rest of the meadow is grown up to pin cherry and perennial herbs (goldenrod, etc.) as it starts its march back to woodland.

At 2.0 mi. the trail begins to rise steeply. At 2.1 mi. white birch and yellow birch are present amidst piles of talus rock. Their angular shape shows they are not glacial erratics but rather have been split off from the bedrock of the upper slopes. At 2.3 mi. black spruce start to appear. The going gets quite steep and is difficult in spots; a good amount of scrambling is necessary. Scattered mountain ash begins to appear.

Finally, after another steep pitch, the 3300-ft.-high summit of DeBar Mt. is reached at 2.6 mi. The foundation of the old fire tower is now all that remains; aerial survey has replaced these towers in most of the Adirondacks. From the top an excellent view is had of the northern Adirondacks and the adjacent St. Lawrence Valley. The tops of the forested hills roll on to the horizon. The land all around the mountain is in the DeBar Wild Forest; the forests surrounding it are the mixture of private timberlands and Forests Preserve that characterize the Adirondack Park. Meacham Lake and Clear Pond are noticed below along with the Deer River Flow. A sense of serenity prevails.

Trail in winter: *Not suitable for cross-country skiing due to steepness of trail.*

Distances: *DeBar Game Management Trail to Baldface/DeBar shoulder, 0.9 mi.; to lean-to, 1.8 mi.; to summit of DeBar Mt., 2.6 mi. (4.2 km). From trailhead, 3.7 mi. (5.9 km).*

(32) DeBar Pond Trail No Map

The trip to DeBar Pond is a short hike through the conifers so prevalent in this section to a hill-fringed glacial lake well known in the area for its trout fishing. This red-marked trail is used mainly by fisherman in the spring.

Trailhead: *Access to this remote trail is from NY 99 4.2 mi. E of its intersection with NY 30. After approximately 4 mi. NY 99 makes a sharp R turn and in another 0.2 mi. a gravel road comes in on the R. Take this road 0.8 mi. to a DEC parking lot on the L. The trail starts across the road from the parking lot.*

The trail begins by going through a cedar swamp on a well-built DEC corduroy plank. It crosses a stream draining the swamp. At 0.2 mi. the plank ends and the trail traverses a balsam fir flat with scattered hardwood.

At 0.3 mi. the trail reaches the shores of DeBar Pond, long and narrow with small mountains jutting above it on two sides; the entire far shore is covered with white birch. In late August the many patches of mountain holly lining the shore are covered with scarlet berries, adding even another little touch to the attractiveness of the setting. There is a private residence to the L at the head of the pond.

Trail in winter: *Generally not suitable for cross-country skiing due to brevity and presence of corduroy plank.*

Distance: *DEC parking lot to DeBar Pond, 0.3 mi. (0.5 km).*

(33) Lyon Mt. Trail Page Map

This trail climbs a massive isolated peak in the far NE area of the Adirondack Park to offer what few mountains in the Adirondacks can—a truly international view. Red-marked, it is the only DEC-designated trail in the scattered patches of Forest Preserve in the immediate vicinity.

Trailhead: *Access to this trail is obtained by taking NY 374 W from Interstate 87 (the Adirondack Northway) Exit 38N at Plattsburgh approx. 23.2 mi. over Dannemora Mt. and around Chazy Lake, above which Lyon Mt. looms, to the Chazy Lake Rd. For those coming from the W, this intersection is 3.7 mi. E of the center of Lyon Mt. village. Turn S on the Chazy Lake Rd. and proceed 1.8 mi. to a gravel road on the R. Take this gravel road 0.9 mi. to its end at the white ruins of the Lowenberg Ski Area lodge. Park here; the trail begins to the L of the lodge ruins.*

The trail starts its steady, strenuous scent to the 3,820-ft. peak of Lyon Mt. by initially following an old jeep road through a second-growth forest of aspen and cherry. This area was clear-cut about a quarter century ago for a ski trail. Before this, the forest was cut over heavily to furnish charcoal for iron smelting in the last century.

At 1.0 mi. balsam fir starts to come in heavily. Shortly thereafter, at 1.1 mi., at an intersection the trail keeps L; the R fork goes to the top of the old ski slope. White birch begins to appear at 1.2 mi. and at 1.3 mi. the remains of the old fire observer's cabin are seen.

The trail continues rising steeply, keeping R at another fork where the telephone wire path goes to the L. The forest is now composed of mature white birch with an undergrowth of spruce and fir. The spruce and fir indicate the composition of the future forest here, while the white birch attest to the severe forest fires that occurred at the turn of the century.

At 1.8 mi. balsam fir becomes the dominant tree in the canopy

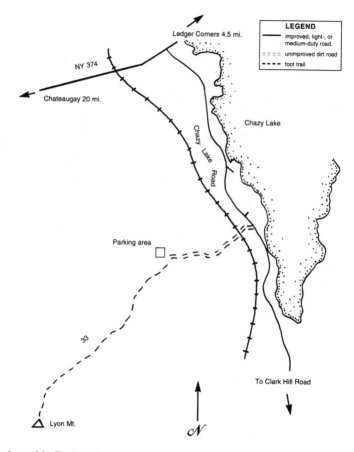

Ledger Corners 4.5 mi.

NY 374

Chateaugay 20 mi.

Chazy Lake Road

Chazy Lake

Parking area

33

To Clark Hill Road

Lyon Mt.

N

LEGEND
improved, light-, or medium-duty road.
==== unimproved dirt road
- - - foot trail

Lyon Mt. Trail (33)
Based on Moffitsville quadrangle

as the winds begin to pick up somewhat. Deer come up to this zone in the summer to use the increased wind velocity to escape the biting flies down below.

At 2.5 mi., after an extra steep pitch, the summit is attained. The fire tower has been abandoned, but was still standing in 1992. The summit is covered with scrubby conifers and mountain ash, as is also the case on the summits of DeBar and St. Regis Mts. These reflect the poor soil and harsh climatic conditions on the exposed tops of these mts. The craggy slopes of Ellenburg and Johnson Mts. can be seen nearby, while the distant High Peaks may be seen to the S on a clear day. That same clear day can provide in addition a view of the skyscrapers in Montreal. Closer by, both the St. Lawrence River and Lake Champlain can be seen, with the Green Mountains of Vermont clearly outlined to the E.

Trail in winter: *Not suitable for cross-country skiing.*

Distance: *Parking area to fork, 1.1 mi.; to remains of cabin, 1.3 mi.; to fire tower, 2.5 mi. (4.0 km).*

Massawepie– Horseshoe Lake Section

In 1991 New York State completed acquisition of two contiguous tracts of land in St. Lawrence County – the 7500-acre Otterbrook parcel in fee and the 19,500-acre Yorkshire parcel under conservation easement. These two parcels, which extend state land from the shores of Cranberry Lake all the way to the shores of Big Tupper and Horseshoe Lake, envelop the headwaters of the Grass River and are part of the proposed Bob Marshall-Greater Oswegatchie Forest. They present especially excellent opportunities for cross-country skiing utilizing the abandoned and active logging roads that travel their length and breadth.

The Otterbrook parcel, which generally lies S of the Yorkshire tract, **is open for full public use except during the duration of the fall deer rifle season** when the hunting clubs that formerly leased the land have retained sole recreational use for a variable period of years. Gates will be placed on the roads leading to their camps.

The Yorkshire parcel was acquired under the innovative conservation easement method under which the state obtains the development and recreation rights and the timber management rights are retained by the original landowner. As this form of acquisition permits the co-existence of public recreation alongside timber and wildlife management, many feel that this strategy heralds the wave of the future in any Adirondack land acquisition. In this particular contract, the state has acquired partial recreational rights for a period of 15 years after which full public recreational use will accrue. In the interim, exclusive private use will be retained by the existing sportsmen's club from the period of the "opening of the deer rifle season until January 1st" and all public use and access will be suspended annually during that time. (The opening of the deer rifle season is traditionally the next to last Saturday in October.) Areas undergoing active lumbering will also be posted off-limits for the duration of the logging. The easement lands are otherwise open to full public use in much the same manner as Forest Preserve lands, particularly with regard to camping, numbers in a party, etc. Any further restriction will be pointed out in the posted signs that delineate the area. Needless to say, the rights of the sportsmen's club should be scrupulously respected for the period they are in effect.

Several interesting long-distance walks through varied terrain and paths are now possible with the acquisition of these parcels. These are mentioned briefly at the end of this chapter. Remember, several of these trails will not be open in the near future for any public recreation for the duration of the annual deer rifle hunting season.

There is a ranger station in Piercefield. The area is covered by the following NSGS topographic map: Piercefield 7.5 x 15-min. series.

For a discussion of recommended hikes, see "Options" at the end of this chapter.

(34) Massawepie-Yorkshire Cross-Country Ski Trail

This ski route makes use of the Massawepie Town Road (a gravel road irregularly plowed in winter) and the main haul road of the Yorkshire Timber Company in coursing through a generally rolling terrain to make a 10.2–mi. round-trip ski tour. If two cars are available, the route can be extended to Horseshoe Lake as outlined at the end of the chapter.

Trailhead: *The ski trail begins at the intersection of the Old Grass River Railroad (now another gravel log road) and the main haul road of the Yorkshire Timber Company 4.9 mi. on the Massawepie Road from NY Route 3, unless the area is unplowed, in which case the ski route will begin at the road junction on the point where plowing ends. Plowing is usually done in winter to a point where the town road ends and the main haul road of Yorkshire Timber begins. After a relatively fresh snowfall, however, the road may be unplowed through the Massawepie Boy Scout section.*

The road (or ski route as the case may be) through the scout camp proceeds for several miles on top of a winding glacial ridge called an esker under a canopy of majestic white pine and hemlock with a number of enchanting lakes and ponds clearly visible on both sides of the ridge. It is, in many respects, as entrancing a ride as exists in the entire Adirondack Park. The Boy Scout camp is open for public use, subject to some restrictions, generally from September until late June.

Beginning (0.0 mi.) at the junction of the railroad bed and main haul road, where cars may be carefully parked to the side, the main haul road proceeds on a rolling course to a gate at 2.1 mi. Ahead lies the caretaker's cabin. Occasionally the road will be plowed to this point. The route goes over rolling hardwood hills,

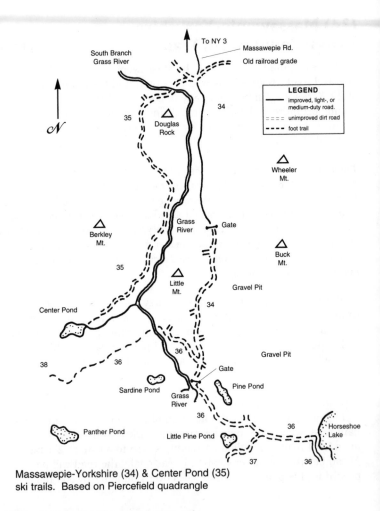

Massawepie–Yorkshire (34) & Center Pond (35)
ski trails. Based on Piercefield quadrangle

with descents in wetland valleys, usually with very obvious beaver activity to the side. Walking here in late summer will disclose a bounteous supply of blackberries and red raspberries by the side of the road.

The caretaker's cabin marks the start of an ascent up a rather steep hill with handsome, maturing hardwoods on both sides along with frequent evidence of deer browsing. Little Mt. is seen for the first time up ahead just before a descent is made at 2.7 mi.

The trail now begins to level out and proceeds through an extensive plantation of Scotch and red pine. The plantation was one of the earlier attempts at reforestation after a disastrous forest fire in the first half of the century. In this case, the plantation was undertaken with private effort.

At 3.2 mi. the trail crosses a wooden bridge and at 3.8 mi. encounters a fork. It turns R here and shortly passes a gravel pit and beaver pond, the latter next to the road on the L. Little Mt. can be seen again.

In addition to the gravel pits, other open areas along the road are the landing areas where logs that are cut are brought for loading onto trucks going to mills.

At 4.0 mi., the route goes L on a grassy jeep trail that turns off the main road, which has been washed out ahead. At 4.4 mi. this trail meets the boundary of the former Otterbrook property (now Forest Preserve) and at 4.6 mi. it ends at a T intersection with another logging road.

Turn R here to another gate at 5.1 mi. The round trip can end here. If two cars are available four more miles of skiing are possible; see the end of this chapter.

Trail in winter: *This trail's primary use is as a winter ski or snowshoe route.*

Distances: *Start of trail to first gate, 2.1 mi.; to fork, 3.8 mi.; to jeep trail, 4.0 mi.; to gate at end of trail, 5.1 mi. (8.2 km).*

(35) Center Pond Ski Trail Page Map

This ski route is a round trip which proceeds over a logging road to Center Pond, generally considered the headwaters of the south branch of the Grass River.

Trailhead: *The trail begins at the junction of the bed of the old Grass River RR and the Yorkshire main haul road at a point 4.9 mi. from NY 3.*

The trail goes R to pass over the Grass River in 0.3 mi. on a small wooden bridge. The river is narrow here but the floodplain of alders is wide. At 0.8 mi. it turns L just before the road straight ahead makes a junction with a road to the R.

The path is wide now with a slight gradual ascent until 2.0 mi. where it begins to undulate. On the way Berkley Mt. is seen across a flooded valley off to the R. The topography of the area is quite obvious in winter—a pattern of wetland valleys and fairly steep mountains looming above them. The road and ski route, however, are generally level to rolling in terrain, a function of the care exercised in laying out the logging roads.

After undulating for a while the road resumes its slow ascent again until levelling off at 3.0 mi. The predominant hardwood forest has fairly good-sized specimens of black cherry and maple with an occasional hemlock. The valley of the Grass River with Little Mt. rising above it is off to the L.

The road begins a descent, turning R at 3.9 mi. with a side road and one of the hunting camps that remain on the L. At 4.2 mi. the road and route end with Center Pond off to the L. Center Pond, with its marshy shoreline and some flooded timber, is quite representative of the many small Adirondack lakes slowly evolving into wetlands.

Trail in winter: *This trail is used primarily as a cross-country ski trail.*

Distances: *Start of trail to bridge over Grass River, 0.3 mi.; to Center Pond, 4.2 mi. (6.7 km).*

(36) Sucker Brook Road Ski Trail Page Map

An enjoyable round trip cross-country ski trip is possible on the logging roads of the recently acquired Otterbrook parcel. These roads, recently used for logging and still used by the hunting clubs who have the option of remaining until 1996, are still in relatively good condition.

Trailhead: *Access is from NY 30 10.0 mi. S of Tupper Lake and 12.0 mi. N of Long Lake. Going W on County Route 421 here takes us to the end of the paved road in 3.6 mi. This is generally the spot where plowing ceases in the winter although, on occasion, plowing may be extended another 1.5 mi. to the former border of Forest Preserve land.*

The trail in the first 1.5 mi. hugs the shore of Horseshoe Lake and makes a sharp L over the tracks of the old Remsen–Lake Placid RR. A number of primitive campsites are available at Horseshoe Lake, a large, deep, conifer-clad body of water shaped like its name. At 1.8 mi., go R at a fork. The gated trail L leads to the Upper Dam at Bog River. At 2.2 mi. go L at another fork. The gated road R leads to Pine Pond and one of the remaining camps. The next fork is encountered at 2.6 mi., where the route goes R. The road L leads to a private inholding. The trail, which has been generally flat, now begins to rise slightly as it passes clumps of regenerating aspen.

At 3.9 mi. there is a junction with the gated Pine Pond road coming from the R at the site of a huge gravel pit. The trail turns L here, passing a logging road on the R which is the terminus of the Massawepie-Yorkshire cross-country ski trail. A steep cliff lined

Sucker Brook Road Ski Trail (36) &
Lows Ridge-Upper Dam Trail (37)
Based on DEC Bog River Flow map & Piercefield quadrangle

James L. Suedberg

Owls Head from North Bay Stream

with spruce stands out sharply to the R.

The terrain now becomes somewhat rolling and the trail descends to cross the outlet of Sardine Pond on a bridge at 5.0 mi. This is considered another source pond of the S branch of the Grass River. Tamarack and alder line the creek. During the summer and autumn months, the gate just before this creek is the limit where vehicles can be driven.

The trail rises sharply up a long hill after crossing the creek and then begins a rather steep descent to cross another small creek with an old beaver vlei L at 6.2 mi. Long Tom Mt., from whose slope the creek flows, is in the background. At 6.6 mi. two of the remaining hunting camps are passed, looking out over an expansive marsh on the L, with Long Tom Mt. majestically framing the outlook. The terrain starts to become rolling again until 7.2 mi. where the trail to Dog Pond takes off R. The ski route shortly ends at an old logging area at 7.4 mi. From this point the trail is narrow and twisting with minimal or no projected future maintenance. It goes on to reach Sucker Brook in about 1.0 mi.

Trail in winter: *Primary use of this trail is as a ski route.*

Distances: *To Dog Pond trail, 7.2 mi.; to end of trail, 7.4 mi. (11.8 km); round trip, 14.8 mi. (23.7 km); end of paved road to RR tracks, 1.5 mi.; to Upper Dam Rd., 1.8 mi.; to gravel pit site, 3.9 mi.; to Sardine Pond outlet, 5 mi.; to vlei, 6.6 mi. (10.6 km).*

(37) Lows Ridge– Upper Dam Trail

Page Map

This hike or ski trip leads to the Upper Dam on the Bog River at the inlet to Hitchins Pond. Looming over the dam and lake and all the early Adirondack history associated with it is a steep ridge with open rock ledges on top where wonderful views of the region can be had.

Trailhead: *The trail starts at 1.8 mi. from the Horseshoe Lake start of the Sucker Brook Rd. ski trail, where a fork to the L (S) is blocked by a gate.*

The trail continues on the other side of the gate. It is generally flat for the whole distance and the roadbed is returning to a natural state although still getting occasional use from one of the remaining hunting camps and DEC personnel.

The trail parallels a vast open peatland on the L for almost a mile. Later it passes a well-drained wetland on the R with a fair-sized creek providing the drainage. The contrast is easily discernible—the peatland with its sphagnum moss, cotton grass and pitcher plants as opposed to the bluejoint grass, alders and pickerel weed of the marsh.

At 1.6 mi. the trail proceeds through the remnants of a Scotch pine plantation with several large talus boulders from the cliff to the R. At 2.5 mi. the entrance to the old Boy Scout camp is reached with the dam straight ahead and Hitchins Pond reached in 400 ft. by taking the road to the L past the abandoned main lodge of the camp.

Just before the gate, on the R between two of the old cabins (or their foundations if they are taken down as scheduled) a ravine is seen. This is the route to the top of the steep ridge that overlooks the entire area. It is 0.2 mi. to the top of the ridge after veering L from the ravine and following a moderately distinct herd path over open rock ledges to the summit. An iron bolt and plaque in the rock commemorate the memory of A. Augustus Low, who at the turn of the century was the lord of all the fiefdom enfolded beneath. Visualize, if you can, the huge lumbering operation employing several hundred loggers housed in what was later to become the main lodge of the Boy Scout complex that in time followed it. Consider also the thriving maple syrup operation in place here, along with the mineral waters bottled from the cool springs and marketed in the large cities on the Northeast. These were due to the dynamism and ambition of the man commemorated. Ponder, too, the scenery clearly unfurling below—the entire wilderness that is the Bog River drainage clearly visible along with the shimmering waters of Horseshoe Lake and off in the distance to the NW on a clear day, one of the Adirondack monarchs, Whiteface Mt.

Trail in winter: *Excellent skiing to foot of ridge at 2.5 mi.*

Distance: *Start of trail to foot of ridge, 2.5 mi.; to top of ridge, 2.7 mi. (4.3 km).*

(38) Dog Pond (from Sucker Brook Road)   Page Map, p. 144

Trailhead: *This red-marked trail is found at mi. 7.2 on the Sucker Brook Road at a point just past a piped spring on the L. The trail begins on the R.*

This is a recently marked trail that leads to an attractive, medium-sized glacial pond where the brook trout fishing can be, on occasion, superb. Access and the beginning of the trail is at the point where a gate on the Sucker Brook Road ski trail bars further vehicle traffic. This point is 5.0 mi. from the end of the pavement on County Route 421 (Veteran Mountain Highway) just before the outlet of Sardine Pond is crossed.

Walk 2.2 mi. along the Sucker Brook Road from the gate, as previously described. A side road descending to the R is encountered here just after a piped spring is encountered on the L.

This is the route to Dog Pond and is marked with sporadic red disks.

The trail goes downslope to cross a creek with wetlands fronting along its corridors. It then enters a tract of cut-over second growth hardwoods until the old Forest Preserve boundary is reached in 0.6 mi. Perhaps nowhere else in the Adirondack Park is the difference between Forest Preserve of long standing and one of recent addition so dramatic. The original Forest Preserve here has not been subject to logging since early in the century and its condition reflects that fact. Majestic hemlock, red spruce and yellow birch point the entire way to the pond. The new acquisition will now start its long path to reach this climax which it will most assuredly do if spared the perils of some natural disaster.

The trail reaches Dog Pond where the inlet comes cascading down a charming small waterfall to merge its waters with that of the pond at 1.0 mi. A number of attractive marked campsites dot the shore area along the way. The trail ahead continues for another 0.4 mi. to join Dog Pond Loop at Proulx Clearing.

Trail in winter: *Generally not suitable for cross-country skiing due to narrowness and twisting layout of trail. Recently cut stumps could also present a problem.*

Distance: *Sucker Brook Road to Dog Pond at Inlet, 1.1 mi. (1.8 km).*

Options

(A) Horseshoe Lake to Massawepie Park. 13.9 mi. (22.2 km). Cars may be parked at County Route 421 3.6 mi. east of NY 30 (10.0 mi. S of Tupper Lake) and at the intersection of NY 3 and Massawepie Road (10.0 mi. E of Tupper Lake). If the road is plowed at the Massawepie end, subtract the mileage the road is plowed from the total.

The first 3.9 mi. is over the Sucker Brook Road Ski Trail to the large gravel pit. After a L here go R quickly and pass the gate that marks the terminus of the Massawepie-Yorkshire Ski Trail and proceed 5.1 mi. to the junction of the Massawepie Road and the old Grass River RR bed (now an active logging road). The road is generally plowed to this spot in winter. If not, it is another 4.9 mi. ahead to NY 3.

(B) Horseshoe Lake to Burntbridge Pond Trailhead (NY 3) 19.3 mi. (30.9 km). Park cars at Horseshoe Lake (described above) and the trailhead for the Cranberry Loop on NY 3 approximately 2.0 mi. east of the hamlet of Cranberry Lake.

The first 8.6 mi. of this walk is on the Sucker Brook Road Trail and the Dog Pond Trail. From the inlet of Dog Pond proceed another 0.4 mi. ahead following the red disks to an intersection with the loop. Go R here and follow the loop 4.0 mi. between Center Pond and Dog Pond Mountain to the trail to Burntbridge Pond. A L here leads to the trailhead in 5.5 mi.

(C) Horseshoe Lake to Cranberry Lake (in the footsteps of Bob Marshall) 19.6 mi. (31.4 km). While attending the New York State Ranger School on Barber Point in Cranberry Lake in the early 1920s, a young Bob Marshall would alight from the train at Horseshoe Lake and embark on a long sojourn through the forest to arrive at his destination – the campus on Cranberry Lake. With a few modifications, the same trek can be made today by an ambitious hiker. Today's hiker will have to be content with arriving at a point on Cranberry Lake a few miles N of the Ranger School, which is open only by special arrangement to the public. The hike will also have to be a round trip, unless a canoe or boat is available on the lake.

From Horseshoe Lake go 9.0 mi. on the Sucker Brook and Dog Pond trails (described above) to the Cranberry Lake junction. Go L at the junction and go W 4.8 mi. to the junction with a side trail to Clear Pond just before a ravine. A L here follows indistinct yellow markers to the shore of Cranberry Lake in 0.3 mi. A vessel will be necessary now unless you decide to retrace your steps 0.3 mi. to the junction. Going L here leads in 5.2 mi. to the Cranberry Lake Loop trailhead described above for a total length (including side excursion to Lake) of 19.6 mi.

Clear Pond
Wild Forest Section

The Clear Pond Wild Forest is a large, isolated Forest Preserve tract located in the far northern reaches of the Adirondack Park. Two recent acquisitions have added considerably to the attractiveness of this wild forest in providing access to a small network of trails.

The Clear Pond Wild Forest is reached from the N by taking George Street in the village of Parishville 5.2 mi. to Clear Pond Road on the R with a stone pillar pointing the way. Access from the S is had by taking the Stark Road R off NY 56 13.0 mi. N of the intersection of NY 56 and NY 3 at a sign indicating Joe Indian Pond. Take the Stark Road 12.1 mi. to the Clear Pond Road on the L. Drive down the gravel road 1.9 mi. to the shores of Clear Pond where a Boy Scout camp complex stood until the inholding was acquired by New York State in the mid-1980s. A number of foundations are still apparent. There is a ranger station in Colton. The area is covered by the following USGS topographic map: Rainbow Falls 7.5-min. series.

Trail Described	Total Miles (one way)	Page
Lilypad Pond Trail	3.3	121
Big Rock Pond Trail	2.9	123
Rainbow Falls Ski Trail	7.6	124

(39) Lilypad Pond Trail

Page Map

This recently marked trail proceeds from the shores of Clear Pond to connect the former Boy Scout lake with three more of the area's glacial gems, whose waters lie neatly folded under the brows of a series of rather steep beech ridges.

Trailhead: *See directions for Clear Pond Wild Forest above.*

The trail bears L at a junction in 0.3 mi. and follows small red trail disks. The initial ridge is only moderately steep and has more beech trees still alive than the other ridges. At 1.6 mi. the trail crosses the outlet of Little Rock Pond. This small pond is quite marshy as the process of eutrophication to which all bodies of water eventually succumb has progressed further here than on the other ponds.

The trail now begins a rather steep ascent and proceeds to cross two ridges clothed mostly with dead and infected beech trees. The culprit here is beech scale disease—a combination of a fungus and an insect. An occasional majestic live sugar maple is also noticed on the ridge. Long Pond is reached at 2.6 mi.; the trail circles one end of the pond passing several nice campsites. Long Pond, which along with Clear Pond is the largest of the area's bodies of water, has many handsome specimens of hemlock and white pine lining its shore.

The trail ascends yet another beech ridge as it makes its way to Lilypad Pond. From the claw marks on the trees it appears that every bear in creation has partaken of the bounteous beech nut crop here at one time or another.

Lilypad Pond is reached at 3.3 mi. Flooded trees are more apparent here than at the other ponds. The trail ends here although marked trees show galore in several directions—a legacy of the time the Boy Scouts blazed trails to their own destinations.

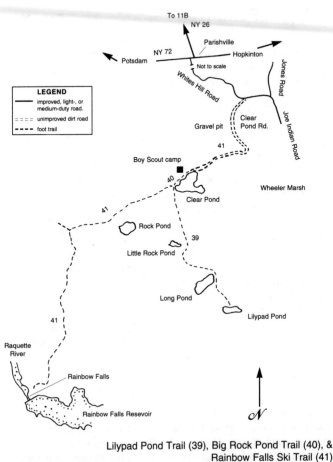

Lilypad Pond Trail (39), Big Rock Pond Trail (40), &
Rainbow Falls Ski Trail (41)
Based on Rainbow Falls quadrangle

Trail in Winter: *Due to steepness, and more particularly narrowness, this trail is not suitable for cross-country skiing.*

Distances: *Clear Pond to Little Rock Pond, 1.6 mi.; to Long Pond, 2.6 mi.; to Lilypad Pond, 3.3 mi.; round trip, 6.6 mi. (10.6 km).*

(40) Big Rock Pond Trail Page Map

Trailhead: *This trail begins at the site of an old Boy Scout complex on Clear Pond and proceeds 0.3 mi. to the fork at the end of the pond. This site is 1.9 mi. down Clear Pond Rd. from its intersection with Stark Rd. (also known as Joe Indian Rd.), which turns off NY 56 S of "The Flats" S of South Colton. Here it turns R and follows snowmobile disks along a wide path.*

The trail crosses a series of hardwood knolls covered with mostly pole sized hardwoods with an occasional conifer. At 2.0 mi. it reaches the outlet of Big Rock Pond. The pond lies 150 yds. upstream and is clearly delineated in autumn by a fringe of golden tamarack encircling the sedge mat around it.

The trail crosses the outlet on a beaver dam and proceeds to a junction with a 4WD gravel road in 2.9 mi. This is the site of the old village of Picketville. Several of the old building foundations are still in the vicinity. A L turn here leads to Rainbow Falls Reservoir—the last leg of a winter ski trip described below.

Trail in winter: *Can be skied in winter as a leg of the Rainbow Falls ski trip.*

Distances: *Clear Pond to Big Rock Pond 2.0 mi.; to end of trail 2.9 mi. (4.6 km).*

(41) Rainbow Falls Ski Trail

Page Map

In winter a lengthy round trip ski jaunt may be made to Rainbow Falls Reservoir using Big Rock Pond Trail as the middle leg of the trip.

Trailhead: *The tour begins where Clear Pond Rd. leaves Stark Rd. (see trailhead description for trail 40) and follows the unplowed Clear Pond Road 1.9 mi. to the shores of Clear Pond.*

The road is gently undulating as it ascends as esker crowned with majestic white pine and hemlock. A conifer swamp is passed on the R before Clear Pond.

The trail now goes R and follows the snowmobile disks on the Big Rock Pond trail to the site of the old hamlet of Picketville at 4.8 mi. There is often a snowmobile base to this point, and a base is even more likely as a L turn is made on the Picketville Rd.

The Picketville Rd. goes 2.8 mi. through mostly Forest Preserve to the shores of Rainbow Falls Reservoir just before the dam. A recent state acquisition has provided access to the reservoir itself at 7.6 mi.

The path is generally fairly wide and the grades moderate but plenty of time should be allotted to complete the trip.

Trail in winter: *The is primarily a ski route.*

Distances: *Start of trail to Clear Pond, 1.9 mi.; to Picketville Rd., 4.8 mi.; to Rainbow Falls Reservoir, 7.6 mi. (12.2 km).*

Grass River Wild Forest Section

With one exception, the trails described in this section lead in some manner to one of the three branches of the Grass River. This attractive wild river is at present little known to the general public primarily because it flows through very little of the Forest Preserve on its north-flowing way to a confluence with the mighty St. Lawrence. Moderate-length, mostly level trails that lead to magnificent waterfalls and scenic vistas provide what access now exists to the Grass River. They are either in the recently acquired Grass River Wild Forest or lead to isolated chunks of Forest Preserve. The five trails in this section are all grouped near the hamlet of DeGrasse. The Church Pond Trail which appeared in the first edition has been deleted because recent road construction on NY 56 has eliminated any parking area nearby along with massive beaver flooding of the entire middle half of the trail. The Big Rock Pond Trail, formerly in this chapter, is now placed in the Clear Pond Wild Forest section with a series of allied trails.

The region is covered by the following 7.5-min. series USGS topographic maps: West Pierrepont (1969) and Stark (1968).

The following trails are included in this chapter:

Short Hike:

Lampson Falls – *0.8–mi. round trip. A walk on a flat woods road terminates at the top of a wide, lovely falls on the Grass River.*

Moderate Hike:

Harper Falls/North Branch Grass River Trails – *3.8–mi. round trip.*
This up-and-down trip is an exemplary tour of northern Adirondack mixed forest and riverbanks.

Trail Described	Total Miles (one way)	Page
Lampson Falls Trail	0.4	126
Grass River Trail	2.2	128
Cascades Trail	1.2	129
Harper Falls Trail	1.0	130
North Branch Grass River Trail	1.9	132
Stone Dam Trail	2.8	133

(42) Lampson Falls Trail   Page Map

Marked with red DEC markers, this trail extends from the Clare Rd. (St. Lawrence County Rt. 27) to the head of Lampson Falls along the main branch of the Grass River. This falls is an imposing 60-foot cascade with a width almost matching its total descent.

Trailhead: *The trailhead on the Clare Rd. is 4.5 mi. from its intersection with County Rt. 77 in the hamlet of DeGrasse. A DEC sign here indicates the Grass River Wild Forest. Park vehicles on the L side of the road and pass around a gate on a truck trail.*

The first part of the trail is a right-of-way through private land until the tall pines of the Forest Preserve are reached at 0.2 mi. Tall white pines and hemlocks fringe the path to the head of Lampson Falls at 0.4 mi. On the L, a short spur leads to the

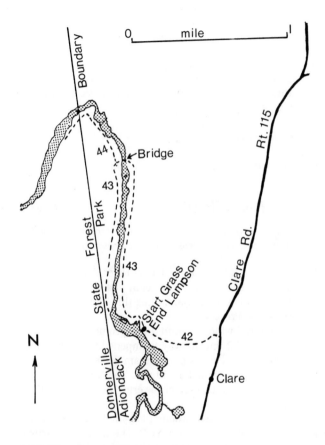

Lampson Falls (42), Grass River (43), and Cascade (44)
trails
Based on West Pierrepont quadrangle

foundation of an old power station that once harnessed the drive of the falls.

The first sight of this falls, particularly after a rain, is truly breathtaking. Many lesser falls have been heavily commercialized. Fortunately this will not occur here with the inclusion of Lampson Falls in the Forest Preserve.

Trail in winter: *Ideally suited for skiing.*

Distance: *Clare Rd. to Lampson Falls, 0.4 mi. (0.6 km).*

(43) Grass River Trail   Page Map

Trailhead: *This trail, marked with red DEC markers, starts at the foot of Lampson Falls. It is in essence an extension of the Lampson Falls Trail.*

It follows along the R bank of the Grass River downstream, then crosses the river and comes back upstream to a bluff opposite the falls. Trails ambling along river banks like this one are relatively rare in today's Forest Preserve.

At the start the trail winds around a low promontory with rock outcroppings until at 0.2 mi. the way is impeded by beaver-induced flooding at a spot where a small inlet stream flows into the river. Hike around this for approximately 50 yds. The trail resumes following the river under a canopy of towering hemlocks on the slope to the R.

At 1.0 mi. the trail crosses a wooden logging bridge recently repaired by the St. Lawrence County YCC. The trail then turns L and follows the river upstream. During the spring the more open forest on this side of the river is carpeted with a gorgeous display of red and white trillium in bloom. Caution should be exercised to avoid the numerous beaver plunge holes that line the bank of the river on this side. At 1.8 mi. a narrow cataract plunges about 12 ft. in a final descent before joining the river.

The trail slowly ascends a bluff crowned with majestic white pine. This excellent informal campsite affords an overlook toward the falls across the river. A path straight ahead leads to a canoe take-out in about 100 yds. This is on the canoe route downstream from the Degrasse State Forest.

Trail in winter: A log road parallels the trail along the river to the logging bridge. This log road, which veers off the Lampson Falls Trail just before the falls makes an ideal ski loop and is used locally for that purpose.

Distances: Lampson Falls to bridge, 1.0 mi.; to bluff, 2.2 mi. (3.5 km).

(44) Cascades Trail   Page Map

Trailhead: The Cascades Trail starts on the W side of the wooden log bridge spanning the Grass River on the Grass River Trail. It is marked with yellow DEC markers.

The trail goes downriver to the end of state land. The return provides a round trip of 2.4 mi.

At the start of the trail, the Grass River contracts from a width of 75 ft. while squeezing through a 20 ft. classic flume under the bridge. This is the start of an enchanting series of nine mini-waterfalls and cascades along the next mile or so of the river. These come in all combinations – some of them in flumes, one even split by a long, narrow island.

The large white pine at the beginning of the trail gradually give way to a forest of mostly second-growth, cut-over hardwoods until the Forest Preserve boundary is reached at 0.9 mi. The next 0.3 mi. of the trail is still on state land, but, as the Adirondack Park boundary has been crossed over, we are now in the Donnerville State Forest. This is a managed forest in contrast to the Forest Preserve, and selective logging is permissible. The trail ends at the start of private lands at 1.2 mi.

Trail in winter: *Generally not suitable for skiing.*

Distances: *Grass River bridge to private land boundary, 1.2 mi. (1.9 km).*

(45) Harper Falls Trail Page Map

This unmarked but distinct trail proceeds from a partially abandoned town road through a recently acquired addition to the Forest Preserve and eventually reaches the foot of an attractive, little-known waterfall.

Trailhead: *Access is from the Clare Road (County Route 27), 7.2 mi. from its intersection with County Route 77 in the hamlet of Degrasse. This is 2.7 mi. N of the trailhead to Lampson Falls on the Clare Road. A dirt road comes in on the L; take it and proceed 0.1 mi. until an old gravel road appears on the R. It is 0.3 mi. along this old road to a gated trail on the L. This is the beginning of the trail to Harper Falls. A trailhead sign and a small, rough parking area have recently been installed here in conjunction with the Unit Management Plan for this Wild Forest.*

The trail passes through some large aspens at the beginning. These are probably holdovers from a turn-of-the-century fire. The trail is undulating at first and then begins a long, gradual descent to the N branch of the Grass River, on which Harper Falls is located. The heavy growth of hemlock beneath the hardwood canopy that lines the cool slopes here points the way to the forest to come. Noticeable, too, are the scattered remnants of the

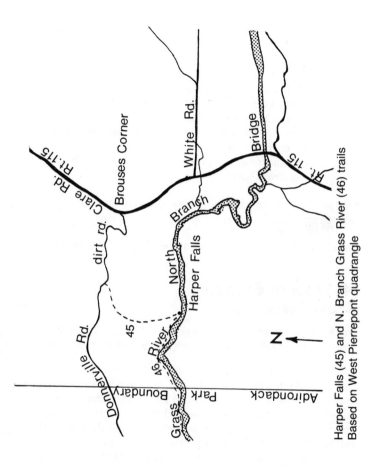

Harper Falls (45) and N. Branch Grass River (46) trails
Based on West Pierrepont quadrangle

subsistence agriculture that was once practiced here. These manifest themselves mostly in the form of old stone walls and barbed wire fences. These agricultural remnants are a rarity in the Forest Preserve of today.

At 0.9 mi. the trail reaches the foot of the waterfall. It veers R another 0.1 mi. where an even better glimpse of the falls is obtained. Harper Falls descends to the floor of the valley in two distinct cascades. The total descent almost equals that of Lampson Falls but the narrow width of the falls, although impressive, lacks some of the grandeur of the much wider waterfall on the main branch of the Grass River.

Trail in winter: *Mostly downhill, twisting. Parking in winter will likely have to be on County Route 27, adding 0.4 mi. to the one-way distance.*

Distances: *Trailhead to Harper Falls, 0.9 mi.; to end of trail, 1.0 mi. (1.6 km).*

(46) North Branch Grass River Trail

Page Map

Trailhead: *This recently constructed river ramble begins at the end of the unmarked Harper Falls trail, 0.9 mi. from the trailhead on the Donnerville Rd.*

Red disks on the R define the trail until it terminates at a truck road in the Donnerville State Forest. Although vehicles may legally be driven to the terminus, the state forest truck trail is better suited to 4WD vehicles. Because of this fact and the relative remoteness of the terminus, it is preferable that the North Branch trail be considered a round trip ramble at this time.

The trail proceeds along the river bank until it reaches the Donnerville State Forest at 0.4 mi. The trail swings away from the river for a while after entering the state forest. The difference between Forest Preserve lands and those of the state forest soon becomes apparent as the trail enters a fairly extensive logged-over area. The brambles and saplings encountered here can be replicated only through natural processes under the ban on logging in force in the Forest Preserve.

The trail soon rejoins the river's bank after a wide circuit of a floodplain wetland and follows it for its duration. In several places it ascends and descends rather steep bluffs above the river as it travels under an attractive canopy of hemlock. Striking specimens of big tooth aspen, close to the maximum size for this early successional species, are a feature of the route. An occasional basswood, a relative rarity in the Forest Preserve, is also seen.

At 1.9 mi. the Donnerville State Forest truck trail marks the end of the trail. The river which the trail has been paralleling is quite attractive, displaying one series of gentle rapids after another. This makes it pleasing visually but definitely not canoeable.

Trail in Winter: *Due to narrowness and steepness in places, the trail is generally not suitable for cross country skiing.*

Distances: *Start of trail at Harper's Falls to Donnerville truck trail, 1.9 mi. (3.0 km).*

(47) Stone Dam Trail Page Map

The unmarked Stone Dam Trail, ~~~~~~~~ ight of way on an abandoned road now u~~~~~~~~ s, provides the only legal publi~~~~~~~~ erve parcel that flanks the middl~~~~~~~~ rail uses this former town road~~~~~~~~ e where a dam erected in connection wit~~~~~~~~ activities at the turn of the century

Note: This trail is not recommended for use at this printing (1997).

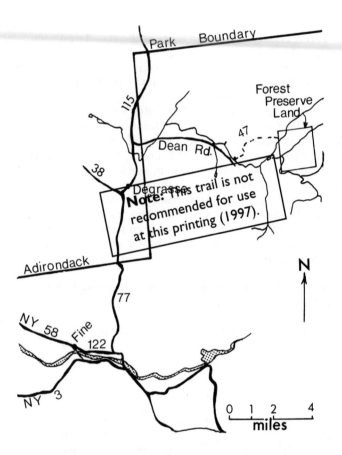

once stood. Grades along the way are mostly moderate, undulating fairly steeply in a few places. In the past, on occasion, the posted signs of the hunting club leasing the adjacent paper company lands have been placed in a position obscuring the start of this trail. However, a careful search should reveal the beginning of the road and the start of the trail.

Trailhead: *From the hamlet of Degrasse proceed on County Route 27 (Clare Rd.) approximately 2.3 mi. to the Dean Rd. just beyond the metal bridge over the Grass River. Turn R on the Dean Rd. and proceed approximately 5.0 mi. to where an old jeep road connects on the L. The trail starts just past the remains of a washed-out bridge on the R. Park vehicles carefully on the side of the road.*

The way at first runs along a pleasant maple-lined lane with the posted land of two large private sportsmen's clubs flanking it on both sides. These clubs, the Rainbow Club and the Stillwater Club, are among the most well known in this region of the Adirondacks. At 0.7 mi. the trail begins to pass through an almost savannah-like terrain with widely spaced black cherry and aspen spread throughout. This is caused by lumbering on these private lands, in contrast to the Forest Preserve lands where lumbering is forbidden. One result of this timber harvesting is that the area possesses probably one of the highest deer populations in the Adirondack Park.

The trail next dips into a hollow where it crosses a creek on a small wooden bridge at 1.2 mi. It continues to a private, wide-surfaced gravel road on the R at 1.5 mi. This is the road the lumber company which owns these adjoining lands uses in conveying the fallen timber from the harvest site to the sawmill. The trail proceeds to 2.3 mi. where another jeep trail crosses it at a R angle. This was the bed of one of the many logging railroads once so common in the area.

At 2.6 mi. Forest Preserve lands are reached. The trail continues straight ahead to the middle branch of the Grass River at 2.8 mi. It then veers L along the river and terminates at a point where a cable crossing of the river still stands. This cable crossing is extremely unsteady and hazardous. Although some of the hunting parties that utilize this remote area in the autumn were apparently still using this cable crossing, it is not recommended.

Only sparse vestiges remain of the old stone dam that was once so prominent here. Much more in evidence are the campsites left by modern-day deer hunters.

Trail in winter: *Suitable for skiing on a snowmobile track but parking is a problem. Dean Rd. is only sporadically plowed in winter.*

Distances: *Dean Rd. to Forest Preserve land, 2.6 mi.; to Grass River, 2.8 mi. (4.5 km).*

Cranberry Lake–
Wanakena Section

The hamlets of Cranberry Lake and Wanakena area at the hub of the hiking trails in this section of the Adirondacks. The former is located at the foot of Cranberry Lake, a widening of the Oswegatchie River whose original size was increased by the erection of a dam. Wanakena, the site of the New York State Ranger School, is located on the Oswegatchie where it begins its flow into Cranberry Lake.

South of these two hamlets an unbroken forest stretches to distant Stillwater Reservoir on the Beaver River. It contains the largest area of virgin forest remaining in the entire NE and the largest trailless area in the state. Both of these are S of High Falls on the Oswegatchie River.

The trail network extends S of the two hamlets and penetrates the Five Ponds Wilderness Area and the adjacent Cranberry Lake Wild Forest. As is the situation with the northern Adirondacks as a whole, beaver flooding is occasionally a problem and a few of the interior trails are somewhat indistinct in their markings. The forest is comprised mostly of maturing hardwoods, with conifers in the numerous wetlands and also on top of the many eskers. The virgin timber of the area is pierced only peripherally by these trails, most notably the Sand Lake Trail.

The trails are generally moderate in grade and lead in most instances to small to medium-sized conifer-ringed ponds and lakes. The northernmost of these ponds have been relatively unaffected by acid rain and still reflect in a general way the excellent brook trout fishing for which the area is famous. Among these bodies of water are Wolf Pond, Sand Lake, Cage Lake, Big Deer Pond, Cowhorn Pond,

Cat Mountain Pond, Glasby Pond, Burntbridge Pond, and, at the center of the woods, the entrancing Five Ponds themselves. There are several prominent ascents: Bear Mt., overlooking Cranberry Lake; Cat Mt., once the site of a manned fire tower and the recently built short trail to the overlook on Dog Pond Mt.

The Darning Needle Pond Trail can be reached only by boat from Cranberry Lake. The Red Horse Trail, reached only by water from Stillwater Reservoir, has been placed in the Stillwater Chapter (Chapter 12).

A DEC ranger station is located in the hamlet of Wanakena. A state campsite is located just outside the hamlet of Cranberry Lake.

Several USGS quadrangle maps cover this large area. They are, in the 7.5-minute series, Wolf Mt. (1968), Five Ponds (1969), Cranberry Lake (1968), and Newton Falls (1968).

Short Hike:

Moore Trail – 4.0 mi.–round trip. An easy walk along a scenic, tumbling section of the Oswegatchie River.

Moderate Hike:

Bear Mt. from state campground – 2.8–mi. round trip. The top offers excellent views of Cranberry Lake, one of the largest lakes in the Adirondacks, and the expansive Five Ponds Wilderness.

Harder Hike:

High Falls Loop – 13.7 mi. This long woods walk incorporates two former logging railroad beds and two foot trails, the highlight being the pleasant setting and lean-tos at High Falls on the Oswegatchie River.

(48) Burntbridge Pond Trail   Page Map, p. 144

The trail to Burntbridge Pond uses the grade of an old railroad bed as do many of the trails in this region. This one, a spur line of the

Grass River Railroad constructed by the Emporium Lumber Company in 1911, was last used to haul logs to the company's sawmill in Cranberry Lake just before the state purchased the land in 1933.

Trailhead: *This red-marked snowmobile trail goes from NY 3 in a SE direction to Burntbridge Pond deep in the heart of the Cranberry Lake Wild Forest. The DEC-marked trailhead is at a parking lot on the S side of NY 3 approximately 2.0 mi. E of the village of Cranberry Lake.*

The trail, currently marked as a snowmobile trail, goes through an area of cut-over hardwoods, crossing several small creeks to arrive suddenly at the junction and trail register for the Bear Mt. Trail (trail 49) at 1.4 mi. and an old, open meadow at 1.5 mi. The creeks all drain into a large spruce swamp to the W and eventually into Cranberry Lake.

Just beyond the old meadow, once the site of a lumber camp, a large glacial erratic of pink granite gneiss is visible. This gneiss is the underlying bedrock of this region.

At 2.1 mi., the trail veers R at a beaver pond. After a bushwhack of approximately 25 ft. around the pond, the marked trail reappears again. At 2.9 mi. it crosses a bridge over Brandy Brook, then proceeds along Brandy Brook under a canopy of hemlocks, passing a designated campsite on the R, until it veers L and arrives at an open glade on the shores of Brandy Brook Flow at 3.0 mi. This flow is one of the flooded inlets of Cranberry Lake. Barney Burns, a famous 19th century Adirondack guide, had a sportsmen's camp nearby.

In the middle of this open glade, a DEC sign on a small conifer points the way L to Burntbridge Pond. The trail straight ahead, marked in blue, is the start of the Dog Pond Loop (trail 50). The trail, which has been generally flat so far, begins to rise moderately, crossing several more creeks on rocks as it ascends a ravine. The forest becomes more mature hardwood, mostly maple and black cherry with some beech.

At 5.4 mi. the blue-marked Dog Pond Loop comes in on the R. The Burntbridge trail continues on a mostly even grade to a fork at 6.0 mi. The trail to Burntbridge Pond veers sharply R, while the trail straight ahead, which is similarly marked with red disks as a snow-mobile trail, goes on to end shortly at the edge of the Emporium Easement lands. At 6.4 mi. another R turn is made away from a similar dead-end snowmobile trail coming in on the L. At 6.6 mi. the trail reaches Burntbridge Pond, circular, marsh fringed, and lined with an attractive mixed forest. The attractive lean-to situated under the conifers adds considerably to the charm of this remote spot.

A DEC lean-to was constructed in 1988 at the end of the trail by the St. Lawrence County Trail Crew with the assistance of the local YCC. The rustic-appearing lean-to, under a towering layer of conifers, gives one of the more striking lakeside vistas in this region.

Trail in winter: The trail makes an excellent cross-country skiing round trip in winter, utilizing moderate grades the entire distance.

Distances: NY 3 to Bear Mt. trail, 1.4 mi.; to Brandy Brook Flow, 3.1 mi.; to Dog Pond Loop, 5.4 mi.; to Burntbridge Pond, 6.6 mi. (10.7 km).

(49) Bear Mt. Trail (from NY 3)   Map: G-9

Trailhead: This trail begins at the trailhead for the Burntbridge Pond Trail (trail 48).

The trail follows the Burntbridge Pond Trail for the first 1.4 mi. to a point just before an old meadow. A trailhead register is located here; go R, downslope, following red markers.

The trail goes through a second growth forest of black cherry, red maple and occasional aspen as it crosses a creek at 1.8 mi. Beaver ponds here are quite attractive but can also cause problems with flooding.

At 2.4 mi. Bear Mountain Creek is crossed on a wooden corduroy. There are actually two crossings, with a sliver of dry land in between. The large, attractive natural boreal wetland that existed here has been reinforced and increased in size with the construction of the dam at Cranberry Lake hamlet. Tamarack, white cedar and white pine make a pleasing spectacle as they brook over the alders and sedges that line the course of the creek.

At 2.9 mi. the trail zig-zags L and then R again to enter a mature mixed forest with occasional hemlock now present. The spruce swamp on the L is the continuation of Bear Mt. Swamp.

At 3.6 mi. the trail connects with the marked trail coming from Bear Mt. Campsite (trail 55). It turns L and follows this trail to reach the summit overlook on Bear Mountain at 4.8 mi.

Trail in winter: Generally not suited for cross-country skiing due to narrowness combined with wetlands and corduroys. Can be done but difficult.

Distances: To junction with trailhead register: 1.4 mi.; to junction with Bear Mt. Campsite Trail: 3.6 mi.; to summit overlook: 4.8 mi. (7.7 km).

(50) Dog Pond Loop   Page Map

Some of the nearly hidden joys of the Cranberry Lake Wild Forest have been placed within greater reach of the hiking public through the recent construction of a loop trail off the Burntbridge Pond Snowmobile Trail. The new trail provides a glimpse of majestic old-growth hardwood stands, secluded glacial ponds and even an historic cave, all of which were previously quite inaccessible.

Trailhead: *This trail begins at 3.1 mi. on the Burntbridge Pond Trail (trail 48) where Brandy Brook Flow is reached.*

The Dog Pond Loop continues straight ahead as the Burntbridge Pond Trail goes to the L at mile 3.0. The Dog Pond Loop is marked with blue disks for its entire distance. It also has orange disk markers for its first 0.3 mi. as it parallels the shores of Brandy Brook Flow. These disappear as the trail jogs L and continues to follow the shore of the flow.

A short walk to the water at any point along the route will reveal an interesting sight—the presence of a number of "houseboats" moored to the shore. These structures, used primarily as camps and in varying states of repair, present a somewhat anachronistic picture, tied to Forest Preserve land and framed opposite Bear Mt., which looms across the flow, in an otherwise pristine, remote setting. They are perfectly legal, however, as the waters of Cranberry Lake and its flows are not considered part of the Forest Preserve.

The loop trail continues to parallel the flow for the next mile, crossing the heads of several small bays under a canopy of hardwoods that gradually increase in size. In this section there are three newly designated DEC campsites on the water to the R. All are attractive, under fringes of conifers with headland settings that feature insect-dispelling breezes. The last one has the bonus of a handsome stone chimney that once graced the premises of the historic Indian Mt. Club.

The trail now veers away from the flow and begins a slow ascent up a moderately steep slope clothed in old-growth hardwoods. Imposing, even inspiring specimens of beech and sugar maple highlight the route; some of the beech have succumbed to the fungus now ravishing the species. This is red tail hawk nesting territory.

At 1.9 mi., after the trail crosses a small ravine, it intersects a yellow trail that leads 0.2 mi. L to Hedgehog or Clear Pond. The first

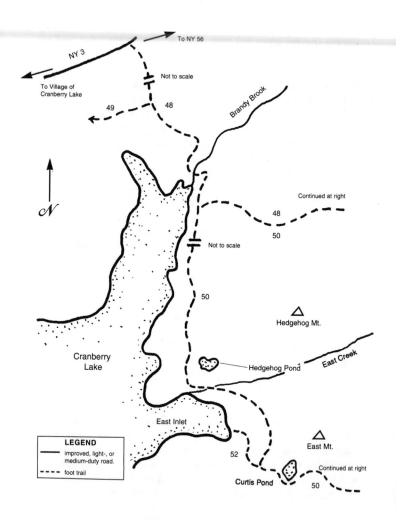

To NY 56

NY 3

To Village of
Cranberry Lake

49   48

Not to scale

Brandy Brook

Continued at right

48

50

Not to scale

N

50

Hedgehog Mt.

Cranberry
Lake

Hedgehog Pond

East Creek

East Inlet

East Mt.

52

Continued at right

Curtis Pond

50

LEGEND

—— improved, light-, or
medium-duty road.

- - - foot trail

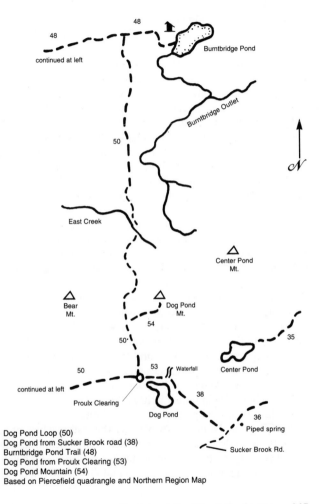

48

48

continued at left

Burntbridge Pond

Burntbridge Outlet

50

N

East Creek

Center Pond
Mt.

Bear
Mt.

Dog Pond
Mt.

54

50·

35

50

53 Waterfall

Center Pond

continued at left

Proulx Clearing

38

Dog Pond

36

Piped spring

Sucker Brook Rd.

Dog Pond Loop (50)
Dog Pond from Sucker Brook road (38)
Burntbridge Pond Trail (48)
Dog Pond from Proulx Clearing (53)
Dog Pond Mountain (54)
Based on Piercefield quadrangle and Northern Region Map

of the glacial ponds along this route, its setting is quite distinctive. Low mountains frame it on one side, and striking glacial erratics lie strewn on its shore.

The blue trail continues straight ahead, passing a designated campsite at 2.5 mi. before descending to the shores of East Inlet Flow and an attractive marked campsite at 2.9 mi. It veers L along this flow, crossing East Creek on a wooden bridge at 3.0 mi. It immediately begins to rise again, crossing a slope graced by truly impressive old-growth northern hardwoods, with yellow birch now joining its companions sugar maple and beech. Many of the beech show evidence of having been climbed by bears in quest of tasty beech nuts.

The loop trail continues its slow climb through scattered glacial boulders. At 3.4 mi. some of these form a rock amphitheater known locally as Willy's Cave.

At 4.1 mi. the loop trail meets the red-marked Curtis Pond Trail from Cranberry Lake, which it follows to Curtis Pond at 4.2 mi. Framed by handsome white pine and spruce on ledges, Curtis Pond is known for its hungry brook trout. A designated campsite is found between the junction and the pond.

Just before the pond, the red-marked trail branches 200 ft. to terminate at the site of a natural rock shelter. This cave is reputedly where Adirondack trapper and backwoodsman Nat Foster hid from a hostile hunting party of Indians in the early 19th century.

The loop trail continues around Curtis Pond, rising slowly with talus slopes on the R. It reaches another of the area's glacial ponds at 4.9 mi. This one, known as Willy's Pond, was previously reached only by bushwhack. Dead timber guards the shore on one side, lending a somewhat haunting appearance to the pond.

Irish Pond is the next body of water the trail reaches, at 5.4 mi. There is also a designated campsite here. Large hemlocks tower over its outlet and a marshy island dominates its center. Like Willy's Pond, this glacial gem was formerly known mainly to fishermen, who bushwhacked in from Cranberry Lake.

At 6.0 mi. the trail comes to a large clearing once the site of Proulx Camp, one of the early traditional lumber camps of the region. During his stay at the Cranberry Lake Biological Center during the 1920s, the youthful Bob Marshall was fond of hiking to this spot. Today the clearing is reverting to forest led by some rapidly grown red spruce, but a beaver flow adjacent to the clearing makes it look large.

From Proulx Clearing, the red-marked Dog Pond Trail goes straight ahead to reach the shore of Dog Pond in 0.4 mi. The Dog Pond Loop goes L at the clearing and begins a mild ascent until it levels off in a magnificent forest of yellow birch and sugar maple. It then begins to rise again as it goes up a draw between Bear Mt. on the L and Dog Pond Mt. on the R following mainly on the lower slope of Dog Pond Mt. At 7.0 mi. the yellow-marked trail to Dog Pond Mt. is encountered on the R.

The trail passes a designated campsite at 7.7 mi. Going straight ahead, the blue-marked loop continues to undulate modestly through a mostly hardwood forest with glimpses of the wild Berkley range of mountains occasionally off to the R.

A stand of large hemlock is passed just before a tributary creek is crossed on a wooden bridge at 9.2 mi. The loop continues to the Burntbridge Pond Snowmobile Trail and terminates there at 10.0 mi. A R turn here leads to the lean-to on Burntbridge Pond in 1.2 mi. A turn L leads back to the trailhead on NY 3 in 5.5 mi., passing Brandy Brook Flow on the way.

Trail in winter: *Generally not suitable due to steepness of terrain.*

Distances: *Beginning on Burntbridge Pond Trail: to junction with Hedgehog Pond Trail: 1.9 mi.; to jct. with Dog Pond Mt. trail, 7.0 mi.; to Curtis Pond, 4.2 mi.; Willy's Pond, 4.9 mi.; Irish Pond, 5.4 mi.; to Proulx Clearing, 6.0 mi.; to finish on Burntbridge Pond Trail, 10.0 mi. (16.0 km).*

(51) Hedgehog Pond Trail

Map: H-9

Trailhead: The trail to Hedgehog Pond (also known as Clear Pond) starts at 2.1 mi. on the Dog Pond Loop.

Turn L at the trail juncture and follow the yellow disks to reach Hedgehog Pond in 0.2 mi.

Hedgehog Mt. broods protectively over the pond as if to guard the wily Adirondack brook trout that dwell in the depths from the ploys of the avid fishermen who constantly seek them out. The trail to the R reaches the shores of Cranberry Lake in 0.3 mi. This point can also be reached by boat on Cranberry Lake.

Trail in winter: Not skiable due to steepness and narrowness of terrain encountered before trail is reached.

Distance: Dog Pond Loop Trail to Hedgehog Pond, 0.2 mi. (0.3 km).

(52) East Inlet Trail

Map: H-10

Trailhead: This short red-marked trail to the shore of an inlet on Cranberry Lake begins at 4.4 mi. on the Dog Pond Loop (trail 50).

The trail proceeds downhill for almost its entire length before reaching the East Flow of Cranberry Lake at 1.0 mi. East Flow is one of the bays of this lake created by construction of the dam at its outlet in the 19th century.

The trail parallels East Inlet Creek and passes under a canopy of towering hemlocks for part of its route. Occasional large hardwoods can also be seen along the way.

Trail in winter: Not suitable due to steepness of terrain.

Distance: *Departure from Dog Pond Loop to East Flow, 1.0 mi. (1.6 km).*

(53) Dog Pond
(from Proulx Clearing)   Page Map, p. 144

Trailhead: *This red-marked trail begins at Proulx Clearing, 6.9 mi. on the Dog Pond Loop (trail 50).*

The trail immediately descends straight down a modest slope. It crosses several rolling knolls covered with large hardwoods until it comes to the Dog Pond Inlet at 0.4 mi. where the waterfall on the inlet cascades down the pond. A number of attractive campsites are located along the shore. The trail continues ahead to reach the Sucker Brook Road in 1.1 mi.

Trail in winter: *Not advisable for skiing.*

Distance: *Proulx Clearing to Dog Pond Inlet, 0.4 mi. (0.6 km).*

(54) Dog Pond Mt. Trail   Page Map, p. 144

Trailhead: *The yellow-marked trail begins 0.9 mi. N of Proulx Clearing at 7.8 mi. of the Dog Pond Loop (trail 50).*

The Dog Pond Mt. Trail goes R as the loop continues straight ahead. The trail weaves up the face of the mountain, encumbered by several large beech lying prone across the path at the beginning. A handsome stand of paper birch, probably the mountain paper birch so prevalent in the High Peaks region, is seen to the L at 0.2 mi. The trail now becomes a narrow path along a steep slope of the mountain. The trail is quite slippery in places, so extreme caution must be used. The trail passes narrow fissures in the cliff and goes under a dramatic rock overhang.

At 0.3 mi. the trail ends in an overlook on the side of the mountain. Part of the view is impeded by a few stunted spruces but an ample view is still had of Center Pond Mt. and Center Pond itself while Dog Pond lies ahead at the foot of several rolling hills.

Distances: *Proulx Clearing, 6.0 mi.; to jct. with Dog Pond Mt. trail, 7.0 mi.; to finish on Burntbridge Pond Trail, 10.0 mi. (16.0 km).*

(55) Bear Mt. Trail (from State Campsite)

Map: G-9

This moderately steep red-marked trail climbs from the Cranberry Lake State Campsite on the shores of Cranberry Lake to the summit of Bear Mt., where unfurls a broad vista of the lake below and of the wild forested hills rolling into the distance.

Trailhead: *Access is from Bear Mt. Campsite Road just E of the hamlet of Cranberry Lake. Take this road S for 1.3 mi. to the campground. The marked trailhead lies another 0.4 mi. inside the campground.*

The trail passes through a growth of mature hardwoods in starting a gradual ascent before reaching a DEC lean-to at 0.8 mi. At 1.2 mi. it reaches a crest of the mountain. The trail proceeds 0.4 mi. along the crest of the hill under a canopy of trees significantly smaller than the slopes. White ash is common.

The trail begins a slight descent before a scenic rock overlook R. State-owned Joe Indian Island is clear, along with privately-owned Buck Island off to the L. At the foot of the mountain, the marshes of Bear Mt. Swamp are visible. In the distance, many of the rolling forested hills appear to be of approximately the same height. Bear

Mt., at 2,520-ft. elevation is, however, one of the highest. Cat Mt., lying due W with its perpendicular cliffs quite noticeable, is slightly smaller than Bear Mt.

The trail now begins to descend sharply for approximately 1.0 mi. to a back road of the campsite. Since it entails walking almost another mile over macadam road to reach the trailhead, most hikers retrace their steps at the scenic overlook to arrive back at the trailhead for a total round trip of 3.4 mi.

Trail in winter: Not suitable due to steepness of terrain.

Distances: DEC Campsite to lean-to, 0.8 mi.; to first overlook, 1.2 mi.; to summit overlook, 1.7 mi. (2.7 km).

(56) Peavine Swamp Ski Trail   Map: F-10

Trailhead: The trailhead is on NY 3 approximately 1.2 mi. W of the bridge spanning the Oswegatchie River on the western outskirts of Cranberry Lake village. A small DEC sign pointing to a rough parking area on the S side of the road can be seen approximately 0.2 mi. W of a state DOT parking lot on the N side of NY 3.

This trail, which skirts Peavine Swamp, an extensive conifer-clad peatland, leads to a secluded lean-to on the Inlet Flow of the Oswegatchie River above its confluence with Dead Creek Flow. The trail rolls over a series of hills and ridges under a canopy of mixed forest with individual trees occasionally attaining heroic proportions.

The trail immediately spans one of the area's many small streams. At 0.3 mi. a trail can be seen going L; this is the Balancing Rock Loop and it may be used as a leg of the return trip. At 0.5 mi. a small wooden bridge carries the trail across another stream, just before a sharp rise to the top of a hill. The forest here is mostly red spruce and balsam fir on the knolls, with tamarack and black spruce joining them in the peatland to the R. Near the top of the hill the forest's composition begins to change to second-growth northern hardwoods with occasional conifers.

The trail undulates through the forest, passing the edge of an old log clearing at 0.9 mi. At 1.0 mi. the Balancing Rock Loop comes in on the L. At 1.3 mi., just past an area of crushed rock remaining from construction, the trail crosses another stream.

At 1.6 mi. the trail begins to ascend a steep ridge. Part way up it passes two impressive red spruces; DEC foresters have measured their DBH (Diameter at Breast Height) at 25 inches, quite imposing for this normally slender species. At 2.0 mi., just after another small creek, the trail passes a hemlock of 40 inches DBH and, at 2.1 mi., one of 42 inches DBH. These hemlocks and the large red spruce may be considered "old-growth" or "virgin" timber, and give some indication of what this area's forest looked like to the early hunters and trappers who penetrated it in the last century. Other equally spectacular giants grew here before the blowdown of 1950.

At 2.6 mi. the trail reaches the top of its steepest hill and begins gradual descent until it joins an old logging road coming in from the L at 2.8 mi. Following the road, it reaches a height of land at 3.0 mi. and swings W at 3.2 mi. At 3.8 mi. it turns L, reaching the lean-to on Inlet Flow at 4.1 mi.

The lean-to is in sound condition, but shows damage from improper use of nails and initials carved into the wood. This is amply compensated for by the splendid setting and scenery. A handsome grove of white pines and hemlock protectively envelopes the lean-to, and the waters of the flow—placid in summer, ice-clad in winter—draw one's attention.

The return may be made over the same route to the old log road or an alternate circular loop to the old log road may be taken.

Distances are approximately the same each way.

Trail in winter: *This trail has been constructed primarily as a ski trail. There are several difficult downhill glides along the route. The route is also somewhat narrow in places.*

Distances: *NY 3 to first leg of Balancing Rock Loop, 0.3 mi.; to second leg of loop trail, 1.0 mi.; to steep ascent and virgin timber, 1.6 mi.; to logging road, 2.8 mi.; to lean-to, 4.1 mi. (6.6 km). Total round trip ski distance utilizing Balancing Rock Loop for one leg, 10.5 mi. (16.8 km).*

(57) Balancing Rock Loop Trail   Map: G-9

Trailhead: *This moderate loop veers L off the Peavine Swamp Trail (trail 56) at 0.3 mi.*

Immediately off downslope to the L as the loop begins is one of the area's hidden jewels: a tiny, dark, limpid pond and encircling peat bog, barely 75 yards away. The trail slowly ascends and descends several moderate ridges as it proceeds along the way. Walking can occasionally be cumbersome because of the stumps still present from the trail's construction.

At 1.9 mi. a sharp turn and loop occur and a slow, steady descent begins. Second growth hardwoods are the order of the day here, with an occasional large beech. Some of the beech are succumbing to the beech scale insect and fungus, but still sporadically produce beech nuts to the delight of local bears.

At 2.7 mi. the trail passes a sharp cliff on the L; it is particularly noticeable in winter. A narrow wooden bridge is crossed at 3.0 mi. and, shortly thereafter, at 3.3 mi., the trail rejoins the main Peavine Swamp Trail. It is 1.0 mi. to the R to the trailhead on NY 3. To the L lies the lean-to on Inlet Flow in 3.1 mi.

Trail in winter: The Loop Trail was constructed primarily as a ski route; grades are generally fair to moderate.

Distances: Start on Peavine Swamp Trail to return on same trail, 3.0 mi. (4.8 km).

(58) High Falls Loop (via Leary Trail)

Map: F-12

High Falls, a scenic cataract nestled deep in the Five Ponds Wilderness, has long been a focal point of hikers in this area. The route has now been marked as a loop with the recently re-routed Plains Trail used to connect the High Falls Truck Trail and the Cowhorn Junction Trail (via Dead Creek Truck Trail).

Hikers traditionally start at the High Falls Truck Trail, and conclude at the trailhead to the Dead Creek Truck Trail. From the Dead Creek trailhead, a walk of 0.5 mi. W is necessary to reach the beginning of the at High Falls Truck Trail. Since the parking area has been enlarged and improved at the Dead Creek terminus, the hiker has an option to begin here. However, for the purposes of this guide, tradition will be adhered to and the loop begun at the High Falls Truck Trail.

Trailhead: Access to the trailhead is from NY at the Wanakena turn-off approximately 8.0 mi. W of Cranberry Lake and 6.0 mi. E of Star Lake. Proceed S approximately 1.0 mi., staying to the R at two forks in the road and crossing a metal bridge spanning the Oswegatchie River. Shortly after, a driveway with a DEC trailhead sign on the R is the entrance to a parking area for approximately 12 vehicles on the R past the tennis courts. A 50-yd. walk on the driveway will take one to the trailhead where a metal gate bars vehicular traffic. The DEC trail register is just past this point on the L.

The trail passes an old mill pond at 0.2 mi. on the L. This is one of the few artificial ponds in this area of abundant natural water bodies. The pond was created in connection with lumbering activities around the turn of the century. At 0.7 mi. the trail crosses Skate Creek on a culvert, then another creek on a culvert at 1.1 mi. Both streams drain into the Oswegatchie River, which is nestled in the depths of the valley on the R.

Just beyond the last creek, the unmarked Dobson Trail takes off to the L. This unofficial trail, the route the owner of a sportsmen's hotel once located at High Falls used in reaching his destination, proceeds through The Plains to arrive at High Falls in the shortest possible distance. However, it is quite difficult to follow in spots.

At 1.2 mi. the trail passes a spring of water coming from a pipe. (These pipe springs, built by early woodsmen, are quite common in this region. Three of them are along NY 3 between Fine and Piercefield). The Leary Trail has been officially abandoned due to the effects of the 1995 "microburst" storm. The truck trail straight ahead is now the way to High Falls.

A path has been cut through blowdown, generally allowing for single-file hiking. The way is rough and bumpy in spots. A large open wetland is on the R shortly after the intersection with the old Leary Trail. The Oswegatchie River lies beyond the wetland over a low ridge.

At 3.7 mi. an unmarked path on the R proceeds 0.1 mi. to the river at a landing called High Rock. A huge glacial boulder overlooking the river bestows its name on the site and also provides a charming and well-known campsite.

The trail continues straight ahead, crossing several streams which on occasion may be difficult to cross because of beaver flooding. The way is generally level as befits the route of an old logging railroad.

At 7.8 mi. the second terminus of the Leary Trail is reached. At 8.0 mi., at a creek crossing, beaver flooding can occasionally be a problem.

The Truck Trail now crosses the W edge of the famous "Oswegatchie Plains" which can be seen L. This unique area, classified as a boreal heath by DEC, is having its blueberry and meadow-sweet shrubs infringed on by sporadic black spruce, black cherry and tamarack trees which are starting to establish themselves.

At 8.3 mi. Glasby Creek is crossed on a wooden bridge with the Oswegatchie River on the R. The trail leaves the Plains to pass the recently rerouted Plains Trail on the L at 8.8 mi. This is a leg of the return trip.

At 9.2 mi. High Falls is reached. A popular campsite, both for hikers and canoeists, the falls present a charming vista as they tumble 20 feet over granite gneiss bedrock under a protective canopy of white pine. There are two lean-tos, one on each side of the river, but the bridge formerly spanning the river has been removed to conform with guidelines of the State Land Master Plan.

The loop returns on the truck trail to the Plains Trail at 9.6 mi. from the trailhead and turns R. The trail goes over wooded knolls with tamarack and white pine lining the way. A large wetland is encountered at 10.0 mi. and crossing can be difficult at times. The re-routed loop is now immediately to the S of the old trail through the Plains itself, which has been abandoned due to repeated flooding.

The trail makes a R swing and runs along the base of Three-Mile Mt. for quite a distance. Several creeks cascading down a ravine from the spruce covered mountain are crossed and a number of large talus boulders are seen in this segment of the loop. The physical location of the Plains, tucked in between Round Top Mt. and Three Mile Mt., gives rise to a situation where frost has been recorded during every month of the year and probably contributes along with other factors to the generally treeless condition of the plains.

The trail swing L away from the base of the mountain and passes the old Plains trail on the L at 11.7 mi. At 12.0 mi. Glasby Creek, now considerably smaller nearer its headwaters, is crossed again and shortly after at 12.2 mi. the loop ascends a ridge and meets with the Cowhorn Junction Trail coming in sharply on the R. This is Sand Hill Junction.

The loop veers slightly L here and begins a long descent down a wooded draw hemmed in by a cliff and ridge on its sides. In summer, due to the presence of leafy vegetation, these are generally not noticed. At 13.1 mi. a juncture is reached with the short Jenack's Landing Trail coming in on the R. A trail register is located here.

The loop veers L and skirts the end of Dead Creek Flow, crossing four small creeks draining off the slopes of Round Top Mt. Dead Creek Flow is the largest of the submerged "arms" of Cranberry Lake that were created by construction of the dam in the last century. Dead Creek itself is crossed on a wooden bridge at 10.6 mi. Several attractive campsites and the remains of a stone fireplace are located here.

The loop now makes a sharp L and begins to follow the Dead Creek Truck Trail close to the shore of the eastern end of the flow. This truck trail, constructed by the CCC during the Depression, is over the path of another logging railroad, and so has quite a level route. At 15.2 mi., beaver flooding has caused a 0.2 mi. re-routing of the trial to the L around the perimeter of the beaver pond. After re-joining the truck trail the loop proceeds L to the barrier gate trailhead erected by DEC at 16.2 mi. From here it is 0.5 mi. L along a paved town road to the start of the loop at the High Falls Truck Trail parking area at 16.7 mi. This can be shortened 0.5 mi. by placing vehicles at the parking areas for both truck trails.

Trail in Winter: A ski loop can be accomplished in winter but has some severe constraints upon it. Narrowness of path, occasional beaver flooding and blowdown, and a few sharp downward twists all combine to make a ski loop in winter somewhat difficult.

Distances: High Falls trailhead to old Leary Trail, 1.8 mi.; to jct. with High Rock, 3.7 mi.; to terminus of Leary Trail, 7.8 mi.; to High Falls, 9.2 mi.; to Sand Hill Jct., 12.2 mi.; to Janacks Landing, 13.1 mi.; to Dead Creek Flow, 14.2 mi.; to start of Dead Creek truck trail, 16.2 mi.; to point of beginning, 16.7 mi. (26.7 km).

(59) Sand Lake Trail

Map: E-13

This blue-marked trail passes through the enchanting Five Ponds to Wolf Pond Jct. on its way to haunting and remote Sand Lake in the heart of the wilderness.

Trailhead: The trail beg_____ of the jct. of the Leary T_____ igh Falls Loop (trail 5___

Note: This trail is temporarily closed as the result of damage from a severe storm in July 1995. For information on reopening, contact your nearest DEC office.

The s_____ and tamarack growing _____ ably prosper in this sterile, sandy so_____ son they are able to survive in the area's bog _____ of competition from the usually more successful hardwoods.

At 0.3 mi., after traversing a conifer swamp, the trail crosses the Oswegatchie River on a wooden bridge. Beaver activity is continual here, so care will have to be exercised in crossing the wet area just before the bridge. This bridge replaces an older one that was washed out by spring flooding. Since this site is deep within the confines of the Five Ponds Wilderness Area, all the construction materials needed were brought in by pack animals to be assembled at the spot.

There are plans not to replace the bridge when it collapses; but as of late 1992 the bridge was in good shape. When, and if, this occurs, Five Ponds and Sand Lake will be accessible only from the Boundary Line Trail (refer to number) from Star Lake through Cage Lake. The conifer swamp of spruce and fir continues across the river and sightings of the rare Canada jay can sometimes be made here. At 0.7 mi. the blue-marked trail makes a sharp turn L at a point where an unmarked hunters' trail goes R to an informal campsite on Wolf Creek. At 1.0 mi. a creek is crossed. It eventually flows into the Oswegatchie River. At 1.2 mi. another creek is crossed on a corduroy plank. The trail then proceeds across a modified esker with the flood plain wetland of Five Ponds Creek on the R.

The trail enters a glen with a babbling brook on the R. Mature hemlock and yellow birch line this glen. The valley is too steep for beavers to dam the brook; consequently, the glen still stands instead of a beaver vlei or wetland.

The trail now turns to cross the creek at 1.9 mi. Caution should be exercised here as there is no bridge for the crossing and it is easily missed. The side of a steep esker is now crossed, crowned with occasional large white pine on top. Generally, these eskers are all considered to be either part of the Cranberry Lake Esker or one of its "tributaries."

At 2.8 mi. the trail reaches Big Shallow Pond where a DEC lean-to is located on the Western shore. This extremely shallow pond is lined with large white pine and its waters have an attractive greenish coloring, unique in this area, unlike the St. Regis area, where this coloring is much more prevalent. Informal herd paths lead over the top of the esker to Big Five Pond and beyond that Little Five Pond in 0.3 mi.

The trail crosses the outlet of the pond and ascends the esker once again. At 2.9 mi. some large red spruce are encountered on top of the esker. There has been some blowdown damage here. The stands of virgin red spruce are not as thick as those of white pine but they still make an impressive sight. Unfortunately, many of the red spruce here seem to be dying; there has been some speculation that acid rain could be the cause of this.

At 3.2 mi. Washbowl Pond is seen L and at 3.4 mi. the trail reaches Little Shallow Pond, where another lean-to is located. Little Shallow, like all five enchanting ponds that have given their names to this entire wilderness area, is a shallow kettle hole lying amidst some of the most magnificent eskers in the Adirondacks.

The trail ascends a ridge after the lean-to and begins to undulate as it proceeds through several small wetlands on short corduroys. Both flooding and occasional blowdown are frequently encountered in this section. The trail then enters a draw with mature hardwoods lining the adjacent ridges, replacing the red spruce and hemlock of the past mile. At 4.2 mi. blowdown is fairly easily crossed after a short distance. An area of small second growth spruce is passed next, and shortly thereafter at 4.7 mi. Wolf Pond Jct. is reached. The trail R goes to Cage Lake (trail 60); the way to Sand Lake is straight ahead.

The trail continues by ascending a ridge crowned with majestic conifers and occasional hardwoods on its way to Sand Lake. The descent from the ridge passes a medium sized waterfall and soon after, Wolf Pond is seen R at 5.7 mi. Beaver flooding may also be encountered in this section along with some blowdown of the old-growth conifers. The trail continues under an impressive canopy of mature conifers until Sand Lake is reached at 7.2 mi. Sand Lake is truly worth the long hike. Encircled by a ring of majestic white pines, its sandy shores beckon the hiker for a refreshing swim.

An attractive lean-to is located R of the lake. An unmarked trail leads over the NW side of the esker to Rock Lake. Equally beautiful and also draining into the Middle Branch of the Oswegatchie, Rock Lake lacks only the magnificent brook trout present in Sand Lake.

Trail in winter: *This trail would make an extremely challenging and scenic ski trip. However, occasional flooding, blowdown and bridge crossings put it out of reach of most. If attempted as part of a backcountry camping trip, careful preparation and caution should be exercised.*

Distances: *Truck Trail to Oswegatchie River, 0.3 mi.; to Big Shallow Pond lean-to, 2.8 mi., to Little Shallow Pond lean-to, 3.4 mi.; to Wolf Pond Jct., 4.7 mi.; to Sand Lake, 7.2 mi. (11.5 km).*

(60) Cage Lake
(from Sand Lake Trail)

Map: E-14

Trailhead: *This yellow-marked trail goes R from the Sand ̶ ̶ ̶ ̶ il (trail 59) at 4.7 mi. It passes Wolf Pond on its way ̶ ̶ ̶ e of the wildest terrain in New Yor̶ ̶*

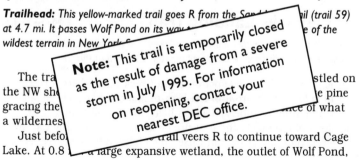

The tra̶ ̶ ̶ ̶ ̶ ̶ stled on the NW sh̶ ̶ ̶ ̶ e pine gracing the̶ ̶ ̶ ̶ ̶ ce of what a wildernes̶

Just befo̶ ̶ ̶ ̶ ̶ ̶ ̶ trail veers R to continue toward Cage Lake. At 0.8 ̶ ̶ ̶ a large expansive wetland, the outlet of Wolf Pond, is encountered. Crossing here can be difficult at times due to flooding; the beaver dams usually present are an aid.

The trail continues to cross the outlet of Muir Pond at 1.4 mi. and then at 2.1 mi. crosses the outlet of Deer Marsh. It crosses several other small creek crossings and wet areas on the way to Cage Lake, but in general this section has more dry area than wet ones. Care should still be exercised in following the disks because blowdown in this remote section frequently is not removed for considerable lengths of time.

Finally the trail ascends a ridge to arrive in 3.3 mi. at the Cage Lake lean-to just before the outlet of Cage Lake cascades across the trail. The trail ahead leads to Buck Pond and eventually the Boundary Trail (75) parking lot and trailhead on Youngs Road in the hamlet of Star Lake.

Trail In Winter: *Due to the remoteness of the trailhead combined with frequent flooding and blowdown, it is not generally recommended that this trail be used for skiing in winter.*

Distances: *Wolf Pond Jct. to Wolf Pond, 0.5 mi., to outlet of Wolf Pond, 0.8 mi., to Cage Lake, 3.3 mi. (5.3 km).*

(61) Janacks Landing Trail   Map: F-11

Trailhead: *This frequently used yellow-marked side trail goes to the R at 10.1 mi. on the High Falls Loop. A DEC trail register is located at this jct.*

It leads to a charming spot on Dead Creek Flow where a DEC lean-to is located. In front of the lean-to is a sandy beach. Small boat traffic from Cranberry Lake is heavy here in summer. Near this site, John Janack, the first fire observer at the nearby Cat Mt. fire tower, had his abode and raised his children in the early years of the century.

Trail in winter: May be skied as a brief side-leg of the High Falls Loop.

Distance: Trail register on Sand Hill Jct. Trail to Janacks Landing, 0.2 mi. (0.3 km).

(62) Cowhorn Junction Trail

Map: F-12

This yellow-marked trail connects the High Falls Loop Trail with Cowhorn Jct. and the series of trails centered on this remote junction.

Trailhead: Access is from mi. 9.2 at the High Falls Loop–Sand Hill Jct.

The Cowhorn Jct. Trail leaves the High Falls Loop at Sand Hill Jct. by going to the L and proceeding gradually up a hemlock glen with an entrancing little waterfall on the R, formed when Glasby Creek cascades down from Glasby Pond. ____ ____ rock than that surrounding it. At 0.4 ____ ____ ____ crossed at the Glasby P____ ____ ____ ____ ____ usually occupied ____

The tr____ ____ ____ making an ideal c____ ____ a short distance u____ ____ to reach Cat Mt. Jct. in 0.9 ____ ____ L here as the Cowhorn Jct. The trail ru____ ____ to begin a descent through a boulder-strewn landscape under a canopy of beech and maple as the cliff-lined shore of Cat Mt. Pond is passed on the L at 1.6 mi. The impressive bulk of Cat Mt. looms above the pond.

Large specimens of yellow birch are now in evidence. The trail encounters sporadic beaver flooding as it crosses Six-Mile Creek and a smaller brook on its way to a short, sharp rise up an esker to Cowhorn Jct. at 2.0 mi.

> **Note:** This trail is temporarily closed as the result of damage from a severe storm in July 1995. For information on reopening, contact your nearest DEC office.

Trail in Winter: *Generally not suitable due to steepness of terrain.*

Distances: *Sandhill Jct. to Glasby Pond 0.4 mi.; to Cat Mt. Jct. 0.9 mi.; to Cowhorn Jct. 2.0 mi. (3.2 km).*

(63) Cat Mt. Trail

Map: F-12

Trailhead: *This red-marked trail starts on the L at 0.9 mi. on the Cowhorn Jct. Trail. This is referred to as Cat Mt. Jct.*

The trail begins a moderate climb through mature hardwoods. At 0.3 mi., the trail begins to rise precipitously as it starts to pick its way up a cliff. After a final scramble, the trail attains the summit of Cat Mt. at 0.6 mi.

From the top of Cat Mt., 2261 feet high, a seemingly endless panorama of forested hills rolls on to the horizon in all directions. No sign of civilization is seen. Three Mile Mt. is the only prominent ridge distinctive enough to be instantly recognizable in the endless wave of green forest. Cat Mt. Pond lies nestled in the valley below. Ravens often circle over it after leaving their nest on top of the mountains. The only remnant of the fire tower that once stood here looking over the horizon is the cement base.

The total distance to the top of the mountain from Wanakena via the Dead Creek Flow Truck Trail is 5.6 mi. one way.

Trail in Winter: *Not suitable due to steepness of terrain.*

Distance: *Cat Mt. Jct. to Cat Mt., 0.6 mi. (1.0 km).*

(64) Clear Pond Trail

Map: G-12

Trailhead: This short blue-marked trail starts at Cowhorn Jct., which is reached by a hike of 6.0 mi. from the Dead Creek trailhead and the hamlet of Wanakena via the High Falls Loop (trail 58) and the Cowhorn Jct. Trail (trail 62). It is at the end of the Six-Mile Creek Trail (trail 66), 4.1 mi. from its start at the West Flow of South Bay.

The trail starts by going R at Cowhorn Jct., following the pine-clad esker until it descends [...] the grade now becomes mostly [...]

At 1.2 [...] glacial pond is f[...] engaged i[...] wetland. T[...] eventually [...] Clear Pond [...] progress fro[...] point. However, an attractive campsite can be found under tall hemlocks on the banks of the pond's outlet in another 0.3 mi.

> **Note:** This trail is temporarily closed as the result of damage from a severe storm in July 1995. For information on reopening, contact your nearest DEC office.

Trail in winter: Trail can be skied with caution but is hampered by lengthy distances from the trailhead.

Distance: Cowhorn Jct. to Clear Pond: 1.2 mi. (1.9 km).

(65) Deer Pond Trail

Map: G-12

Trailhe[...] [...]lly in evidence [...] [...]m the Clear Pon[...]

> **Note:** This trail is temporarily closed as the result of damage from a severe storm in July 1995. For information on reopening, contact your nearest DEC office.

The trail descends slightly at the start and proceeds through a forest of mostly medium-sized hardwoods, arriving at an open glade with raspberries and blueberries at 0.6 mi. The trail passes tiny Grassy Pond L at 0.8 mi., then begins to climb to the top of an esker at 1.0 mi. The trail descends past Sl~~en~~ ~~is~~ s seen L at 1.3 mi. This small pond lying i~~n~~ narrow at the waist and the~~n~~ completely encircle~~d~~

At 1.5 ~~~~ nofficial hunter's t~~~~ an old spirea-co~~~~ n to the L.

At 2.1 ~~~~ Big Deer Pond lies straight ah~~~~ ~~and~~ shallow lake with emergent grassy vegetation p~~~~ ~~ding~~ in many areas. Due to the abundance of deer, this was a favorite spot for hunters to be flown in before the classification as wilderness.

> **Note:** This trail is temporarily closed as the result of damage from a severe storm in July 1995. For information on reopening, contact your nearest DEC office.

Trail in Winter: *A lengthy ski-advised only with extreme caution and detailed preparation and planning.*

Distances: *Cowhorn Jct. to Grassy Pond, 0.5 mi.; to Slender Pond, 1.3 mi.; to Big Deer Pond, 2.1 mi. (3.4 km).*

(66) Six-Mile Creek Trail   Map: G-11

Trailhead: *This trail begins at Cowhorn Jct. and ends on the W flow of South Bay in Cranberry Lake. If the trail is started from the lake, it is approximately 5.0 mi ~~~~ ~~ke~~ outside ~~~~*

> **Note:** This trail is temporarily closed as the result of damage from a severe storm in July 1995. For information on reopening, contact your nearest DEC office.

The trail follows blue markers on top of an esker for 0.2 mi. where a yellow-marked side trail comes in R. This leads in a short while to a lean-to at Cowhorn Pond (see above).

The trail continues on top of the esker until it reaches a second esker branching off to the L at 0.4 mi. Many of the eskers in this area show their relationship to the under-ice streams from which they originated by flowing into each other.

At 1.0 mi., the trail makes a descent and wetlands are noticed on both sides. The outlet of Cowhorn Pond is on the R while Six-Mile Creek, the outlet of Bassout Pond, is on the L. The trail ascends an esker again and passes a large open wetland with beaver ponds L at 1.9 mi. At 2.1 mi., Tamarack Bog comes into view on the L. Pitcher plants are particularly abundant here.

At 2.3 mi., the trail goes through a yellow birch and hemlock forest while still hugging the top of the esker. This esker is called the Cranberry Lake Esker by geologists. Large white pine and medium spruce grow on top here. At 2.7 mi., at a jct., the obscure trail R, now officially abandoned, leads to Ash Pond; the yellow-marked Olmstead Pond Loop goes L. The trail then dips down to pass an abandoned beaver flow on the R before sharply ascending another esker at 2.9 mi. A huge glacial erratic with young birch and polypod fern growing on it is prominent on top.

At 3.3 mi., the trail passes Sliding Rock Falls on Six-Mile Creek on the L. This falls is as high as High Falls but has considerably less water volume. The trail then goes on to reach a DEC trail register at 3.7 mi. An unmarked trail R goes to the E flow of South Bay and provides access to private inholdings.

The trail passes mostly hardwoods as it arrives at the W flow of South Bay at 4.1 mi. Indian Mt. looms above the trail on the R. At its foot nestles Indian Mt. Pond, now reached only by a bush-whack, but once the site of a famous sportsmen's club before state purchase of the land for inclusion in the Forest Preserve. It is approximately 5.0 mi. by boat from here to the DEC launching site at Cranberry Lake village.

Trail in winter: *Can be skied but twisting and narrow in places. Remoteness also a factor.*

Distances: *Cowhorn Jct. to junction with Olmstead Pond Trail, 2.7 mi.; to Sliding Rock Falls, 3.3 mi.; to Cranberry Lake, 4.1 mi. (6.6 km).*

(67) Cowhorn Pond Trail

Map: G-12

Trailhead: *This short side trail goes R at 0.2 mi. from Cowhorn Jct. along the Six-Mile Creek Trail (trail 66). It is marked with yellow disks.*

The trail makes a moder~~ate~~ n-to on a point of this ha~~rd~~ from its resembla~~nce~~ in the summer

> **Note:** This trail is temporarily closed as the result of damage from a severe storm in July 1995. For information on reopening, contact your nearest DEC office.

Trail in wi~~nter~~ ~~ski loop~~ from the trailhead in ~~Wanakena.~~

Distances: ~~Six-Mile~~ Creek Trail to Cowhorn Pond, 0.2 mi. (0.3 km).

(68) Olmstead Pond Loop

Map: G-11

Trailhead: *This pond visiting loop, which can be wet in spots, leaves the Six-Mile Creek Trail (trail 66) at mi. 2.7. Follow the yellow disks to the L.*

The trail starts to descend at 0.1 mi., becoming muddy with running rivulets, especially after a rain. At 0.3 mi., the trail crosses Six-Mile Creek and runs alongside it briefly. The forest is of mixed hemlock and hardwoods. Six-Mile Creek is spanned again at a difficult crossing, the bridge having been washed out by flooding.

The trail then begins to climb, with the outlet of Olmstead Pond on the L, cascading down to join Six-Mile Creek below. At 0.7 mi., Olmstead Pond is reached. The outlet waters here have been dammed by beavers.

The old trail to Olmstead Pond ended at this juncture. The trail has now been extended to make a loop re-joining the Six-Mile Creek Trail after passing Simmons and Spectacle ponds.

After reaching Olmstead Pond, the trail works its way around the S shore of the pond to reach the lean-to at the pond's head in 1.2 mi. The lean-to receives frequent usage, especially in fishing season.

The trail skirts the shores of Olmstead Pond and Simmons Pond. At 1.6 mi. a short marked side trail leads in 150 yds. to the outlet of Simmons Pond just past where it leaves the pond. Simmons Pond, with its hardwoods and occasional white pine on the shore, is one of the relatively few water bodies in the area characterized by a greenish-blue coloring. The minerals in the water give it this attractive look, in contrast to the usual brownish-grey of the typical Five Ponds Wilderness bodies of water.

The trail now loops around Olmstead Pond and begins to ascend steadily. At 2.1 mi. the trail descends quite steeply to the shore of Spectacle Pond. Continuing past the pond, the loop proceeds through a generally mixed forest to rejoin the Six-Mile Creek Trail at 3.2 mi., 1 mi. N of the first leg.

Trail in winter: *Generally not suitable for winter skiing due to steepness of terrain.*

Distances: *Six-Mile Creek Trail to Olmstead Pond lean-to, 1.2 mi.; to side trail to Simmons Pond, 1.6 mi.; to Spectacle Pond, 2.1 mi.; to end of loop back on Six-Mile Creek Trail, 3.2 mi. (5.1 km).*

(69) Darning Needle Pond Trail   Map: H-11

This trail can best be reached by boat from Cranberry Lake.

Trailhead: *The best access to this yellow-marked trail is by boat to the point on South Bay where Chair Rock Creek empties into Chair Rock Flow. Chair Rock Creek is the outlet of Darning Needle Pond and the trail generally runs parallel with the creek until it reaches the pond. Access may also be had via an unmarked foot trail leading from the beginning of the Six-Mile Creek Trail at the head of West Flow, the other flow of the South Bay. This trail, which is partially on private land near several lakeshore camps, leads in approximately 1.5 mi. to the start of the Darning Needle Pond Trail.*

The trail begins to rise steadily through pole-sized hardwoods as it parallels the creek. As this trail is remote, regular maintenance is difficult and beaver flooding can occasionally be a problem. At 0.8 mi., it passes rapids along the creek with a small attractive waterfall in one spot. The valley of this short creek is relatively wide and has beaver-created wetlands in quite a few places along it course.

At 1.9 mi., the trail crosses the creek on a beaver dam and proceeds along a bluff overlooking fairly extensive wetlands until it reaches the shores of Darning Needle Pond at 2.6 mi. Darning Needle, long and narrow, has its shore ringed with a mixture of conifers and hardwoods with several low hills ringing the pond on the S.

Trail in Winter: *Not suitable for skiing due to remoteness of setting, numerous creek crossings and wetness which could prove difficult and dangerous.*

Distance: *Cranberry Lake to Darning Needle Pond, 2.6 mi (4.2 km).*

(70) Headwaters Canoe Carry   Map: G-13

This remote canoe carry linking the headwaters of the Bog and Oswegatchie rivers is the ultimate in a wilderness trail. The carry is in two stages: from Bog River to Big Deer Pond, then from Big Deer Pond to the upper reaches of the Oswegatchie River.

Trailhead: The trail starts on the W bay of Lows Lake, which is the extension of the Bog River, at a canoe carry sign on a south peninsula. This point is reached after a paddle of approximately 15.0 mi. from the put-in at the Bog River lower dam (see trail 5).

The trail starts by following the yellow canoe carry disks to an intersection with an old log road at 0.4 mi. Veer R on the wider log road and follow the yellow disks through a second growth hardwoods to arrive at the canoe put-in on the N shore of the Big Deer Pond at 0.9 mi.

The canoe carry trail resumes on the W shore of Big Deer Pond, where the yellow disks start again. A paddle can be made here, or a bushwhack of 0.5 mi. can be made westerly around the Pond until the disks are seen again.

The carry crosses the outlet of Deer Pond at 2.0 mi. Planks are present in this flooded area but occasionally the crossing will have to be made using a beaver dam. The trail proceeds to rise and cross over the top of another steep hill, one of the area's numerous eskers, at 2.9 mi. This esker, according to DEC measurements, is 180 feet high from base to top.

The trail descends and begins a long, steady course to the shores of the Oswegatchie River at a point below the area referred to as Beaver Dam at 3.5 mi. Large white pine are present in this last section and a DEC campsite is on the bank of the river.

Trail in Winter: *Mainly due to the extreme remoteness of the trail, this canoe carry is not suitable for cross-country skiing in winter.*

Distances: *Lows Lake to Big Deer Pond, 0.9 mi.; bushwhack around Big Deer Pond to resumption of carry on SW shore, 1.4 mi.; to terminus of trail at Oswegatchie River, 3.5 mi. (5.6 km).*

(71) Old Wanakena Road Trail   Map: E-11

This red-marked snowmobile trail through the Cranberry Lake Wild Forest began as one of the many logging railroads in the area. It subsequently became a motor vehicle road, at one time the only road to Wanakena. It was then abandoned, with the last car traveling on the road in the 1930s.

Trailhead: *Access to the trail is from the Wanake̶ ̶ ̶ ̶ ̶d at a point on the R 0.4 mi. from its junction with NY 3. T̶ ̶ ̶ ̶ ̶ ̶ t the beginning, with a metal barrier preve̶ ̶ ̶ ̶*

Note: This trail is currently (summer 1997) impassable as a result of beaver flooding.

The trail pr̶ ̶ ̶ ̶ ̶ ̶ ̶ ̶ e plantation on lands of the Ne̶ ̶ ̶ ̶ ̶ ̶ ̶ ̶or. A 0.3 mi., it reaches the Forest Pres̶ ̶ ̶ ̶ ̶ ̶ns sharply L following red DEC markers. The trail straight ahead goes to NY 3 in about one mi.

The trail crosses several small creeks before coming to an area so persistently flooded by beaver that, at 0.8 mi., it has been rerouted for 0.2 mi. up a slope adjacent to the flooded area. The detour rejoins the main trail at 1.0 mi. and continues to parallel the brook until 1.4 mi. where the trail and brook part company.

The forest is of moderate-sized hardwoods and hemlocks, a reflection of the heavy logging that occurred here early in the century.

At 2.1 mi., a gravel pit, which furnished much of the material for the old road, appears on the R. The trail then goes through mostly second-growth hardwoods on a wide grassy path to reach the Inlet Road at 2.4 mi. A R turn on the Inlet Road leads to NY 3 in 2.4 mi. A L will bring one past the Moore Trail terminus (see below) to Inlet Landing in 0.7 mi.

Trail in Winter: *Trail may be done as a cross-country ski round trip taking care when crossing bridges and small creeks. The slight detour in trail to avoid beaver flooding is quite steep and could prove difficult.*

Distance: *Wanakena Road to Inlet Road, 2.4 mi. (3.8 km).*

(72) Moore Trail   Map: E-11

Trailhead: *Access to this yellow-marked trail is from the Wanakena Road, approximately 1.0 mi. from NY 3 just before the metal bridge crossing the Oswegatchie River. A DEC trail sign can be seen on the R. From here, it is less than 0.1 mi. to the trailhead for the High Falls Loop.*

The trail goes behind a private residence to proceed along the banks of the Oswegatchie River until the Inlet Landing canoe launch site. The start of the trail presents a view of many large boulders in the riverbed. The rapids along the two-mile stretch of river make it unsuitable for canoeing but contribute to a splendid view from the trail along the bank, as the many cataracts and pools are almost continually in sight. In early springs, the painted trillium in bloom under the tall conifers of hemlock, spruce and balsam fir also present a pretty picture.

At 1.0 mi. the trail passes a series of small waterfalls. At 1.3 mi. a charming beaver pond is seen R. Beavers have a tendency to dam small creeks just as they enter a main river. Shortly thereafter, a number of white cedars are encountered on the river-bank. The arbutus or mayflower also blooms here in the spring. At 2.0 mi. the trail reaches Inlet Road after crossing a sliver of private land.

A short walk on the road to the L leads to the Inlet Landing. From here, the river is passable by canoe to its upper reaches. The landing was once the site of a sportmen's hotel. The trail is named after one of the early hotel proprietors.

Trail in Winter: *Can be skied as a round trip of 4.0 mi. Narrow in places.*

Distance: *Wanakena to Inlet Road, 2.0 mi. (3.2 km).*

Star Lake–
Streeter Lake Section

The regional center of Star Lake together with outlying Streeter Lake forms the nucleus of the hiking trails in this section of the Adirondack Park. The trails travel in a generally S direction from Star Lake village and then form a network running E and W. In many cases the trails interconnect and offer a series of circuits in addition to the basic round trips. The trails go mainly through the Aldrich Pond Wild Forest, and in a few instances penetrate deeply into the Forest Preserve, allowing the additional option of extended round trips. Grades are mostly moderate and usually lead through second-growth hardwood forests with dense conifer swamps and beaver flows present more often than not in low-lying areas. As in the adjoining Cranberry Lake section, these beaver-flooded areas along the trail fluctuate widely in their presence contingent on food supply, predation and fur harvesting.

The destination of these trails is often one of the myriad small jewel-like ponds that lie scattered in enchanted, remote hollows throughout the region. Some of these are Round Lake, Long Lake, Scuttle Hole Pond, Streeter Lake, Crystal Lake, Buck Pond, Little Otter Pond, and Cage Lake. On the E these trails connect with the trail system emanating from the Cranberry Lake-Wanakena Section. This gives ultimate access to the virgin timber of the remote sections of the Five Ponds Wilderness Area. There are no ascents of mountains with views, although the wooded shoulders of a few moderate-sized hills are crossed over.

There are a number of changes since the first edition. The Jakes Pond trail has been placed in the new Watsons East Triangle

Chapter (Chapter 11). The Gulf Trail in the first edition, being unmarked and subject to blowdown, is now best considered as a bushwhack. Finally, the Alice Brook and Pins Creek trails have been deleted, the former because it is now difficult to reach the changed trailheads for the Buck Pond-Cage Lake Trail and the latter due to heavy beaver flooding and abandonment by DEC. A few other trails have been incorporated as segments of longer trails.

A DEC Ranger Station is located in the town of Pitcairn. The region is covered by the following USGS topographic maps: 7.5 minute series: Oswegatchie, Oswegatchie Southwest (1966), Oswegatchie Southeast (1966).

Moderate Hike:

Streeter Lake from Youngs Road – *7.0–mi. round trip. A hike on a snowmobile trail ends at historic and mysterious Streeter Lake.*

Harder Hike:

Cage Lake via Boundary Trail – *14.6–mi. round trip. Deep in the Five Ponds Wilderness Area, Cage Lake gives one a true wilderness feeling.*

Trail Described	Total Miles (one way)	Page
Little River Trail	0.8	177
Streeter Lake (from Youngs Rd.)	3.5	179
Cage Lake (via Boundary Trail)	7.3	181
Round Lake (from Aldrich)	3.4	183
Round Lake (from Kalurah)	5.0	185
Streeter Lake Ski Trail (from Aldrich)	4.7	187
Middle Branch Oswegatchie Trail (via Totten-Crossfield)	5.6	189

(73) Little River Trail

Formerly the Streeter Lake Trail from Amo Rd., this trail was laid out as a cross-country ski route by the St. Lawrence County YCC. A yellow-marked DEC trail, it originally proceeded from the outskirts of Star Lake village in a generally SW direction to arrive at a DEC lean-to located on a bluff overlooking the shores of Streeter Lake.

Since the second edition, the wooden bridge spanning the Little River at 0.8 mi. has been removed by the DEC. At present, there are no plans to replace it. Because the crossing of the Little River at this junction is quite hazardous, the tr____ ends at this point.

Trailhead: _____ e. Turn S off NY 3 at it_____ ke and proceed 0.3 m_____ and proceed 0.1 m_____ to the trailhead sign on the L in 0.6 mi.

Note: This trail has been officially abandoned. For nearby access to the Little River, see "Attention!" on page vi in the Preface.

The trail at the start crosses some of the typical glacial knolls that dot the region before descending into a long, narrow hollow. At 0.3 mi. the trail ascends one of these knolls where it intersects with a jeep trail. The trail goes straight ahead here with a little veer to the L until it reaches a ridge overlooking the floodplain marshes of the Little River at 0.6 mi.

After running along the ridge for a while the trail descends to where the bridge once spanned the Little River. The trail now culminates at this spot.

Trail in winter: The brevity of the trail limits its appeal for cross-country skiers.

Distances: Amo Rd. to Little River, 0.8 mi.

(74) Streeter Lake
(from Youngs Rd.)

This DEC red-marked snowmobile trail presents an alternate and somewhat shorter route to Streeter Lake than the Amo Rd. Trail from Star Lake village. Access is from the Youngs Rd. over a recently acquired Forest Preserve parcel. This is approximately 1.0 mi. by road from the Amo Rd. trailhead.

Trailhead: To reach the trailhead, proceed on Youngs Rd. from its junction with NY 3 in the center of Star Lake. The trailhead is on the R at 1.4 mi. from NY 3, just after a metal bridge across the Little River. A gated jeep trail is the beginning of this trail.

The trail proceeds through pole-sized black cherry to a wooden bridge across Tamarack Creek at 0.3 mi. Just before the crossing an old log road comes in on the L and joins the snowmobile trail. This is a marked horse trail which leads in 0.4 mi. to a trailhead on Youngs Rd. at a point 0.2 mi. S of the snowmobile trailhead. Tamarack Creek is now entirely in the Forest Preserve from its remote headwater springs near the Herkimer County line to its confluence with the Little River 300 yds. downstream from the bridge.

The trail now goes through medium-sized spruce and fir that

have seeded in on the hayfields that were once on this site. These were used to raise feed for the horses that were once used in connection with the logging industry. The trail goes R at a fork and shortly thereafter at 0.7 mi. goes L at another fork. At 0.8 mi. a small field of spirea is a holdover from the old hayfields; apparently the thick growth of the spirea plus the fact that the field is in what appears to be a low-lying frost pocket has hindered the regrowth of forest in this one small section.

At 1.0 mi. a red-marked snowmobile trail years in sharply from the R to join this trail. Snowmobile trail markers mark the route from here to the old Potato Patch. At 1.1 mi. the trail passes a hunting camp on a private inholding on the L and at 1.2 mi. it enters a Scotch pine plantation. At 1.3 mi. the trail goes R at a jct. and shortly thereafter passes a log road on the R. This was the beginning of the old link trail which previously connected the two Streeter Lake trails from Amo and Youngs roads. A few of the metal posts for the underground telephone wires that once serviced the large private estate are still seen standing here. The trail now becomes moderately steep and the wooded top of Streeter Mt. can be seen clearly outlined ahead at 2.3 mi.

The trail crosses the outlet of Streeter Lake on a bridge at 2.7 mi., and shortly thereafter climbs over the shoulder of Streeter Mt. At 2.9 mi. the old yellow state boundary markers are passed; the rest of the trail is now entirely within what was originally the Schuler estate. The trail goes ahead until the yellow markers of the amo Road ski trail appear on the R at 3.1 mi. These trails now run concurrently to the old Potato Patch at 3.3 mi. Directly W across the Potato Patch, Streeter Lake and its lean-to are reached at 3.5 mi.

Trail in winter: *Suitable for skiing.*

Distances: *Youngs Rd. to outlet of Streeter Lake, 2.7 mi.; to Amo Trail, 3.1 mi.; to Potato Patch, 3.3 mi.; to Streeter Lake, 3.5 mi. (5.6 km).*

(75) Cage Lake
(via Boundary Trail)

Map: D-12

Trailhead: *With the removal of the Oswegatchie River bridge at Cage Lake Springhole, the shortest route to Cage Lake is now from the village of Star Lake via the newly marked Boundary Trail, and then over the bed of the old Post Henderson logging RR past Buck Pond. A new parking area has been built by the St. Lawrence County YCC on the Youngs Rd. 1.9 mi from NY 3, approximately 0.5 mi S of the previous trailhead for the Buck Pond trail described in the first edition. This new trailhead not only shortens the distance to Cage Lake but also avoids most of the ruts encountered in the first 2.0 mi. of the old Buck Pond Trail, which was not on the RR bed.*

The trail, marked with yellow disks for the first 0.6 mi., begins at the parking area to the L on Youngs Rd. It slowly begins an ascent as it undulates through a mature forest featuring splendid specimens of hemlock, yellow birch, and black cherry interspersed with occasional large glacial erratic. The yellow paint on the trees along the trail indicates what was formerly the boundary between Forest Preserve and private land. With state acquisition of the Pine Pond parcel in 1989, now only the name of the trail itself is relevant.

At 0.6 mi. the trail goes L as it starts to follow a jeep trail marked with red disks. At 1.1 mi. the old Buck Pond trail comes in on the L and, shortly thereafter, the bed of the old logging RR is joined. It is followed almost the entire distance to Buck Pond.

The trail proceeds through a pole-sized hardwood forest, arriving at Little Otter Pond at 2.1 mi.

Little Otter, hardwood-fringed with a number of beaver lodges on its banks, is one of the typically shallow ponds of this region. The trail crosses the outlet of Little Otter Pond at 2.3 mi. and a balsam-lined beaver vlei at 3.1 mi. The beaver have long gone from here and the vlei that succeeded the open water or flow is in turn being replaced by the encroaching forest.

At 3.4 mi. the outlet of Little Otter is crossed again; it has made a meandering turn on its way toward its final flow into Tamarack Creek. The trail continues to a difficult crossing at the site of beaver flooding at 4.9 mi. It is necessary to bushwhack to the R around the flow here.

At 5.3 mi the old railroad bed turns R while the Buck Pond Trail keeps to the L. A gate barring further ATV travel has been placed across the RR bed here.

The trail now begins to rise again rather sharp and a hill crowned with tall hemlocks is crossed at 6.1 mi. The trail then begins a slow, gradual descent to reach the shores of Buck Pond at 7.3 mi. The trail R just before the pond leads to Cage Lake and ultimately to the trail network beginning at Wanakena.

Buck Pond, approximately the same size as Little Otter Pond, is rimmed with both hardwood and conifers. There is an interesting glacial erratic just before the shore. This large boulder is composed of reddish granitic gneiss, the same composition as the underlying bedrock here. The two small camps of the private inholding are located at the head of the lake. The trail to Cage Lake makes a sharp R turn just before Buck Pond.

The trail, now marked with yellow disks, continues to an intersection wi[th ...]hole trail at 7.6 mi. on the L. T[...]ning the Oswegatchie R[...]e followed only with difficulty.

Note: This trail now terminates at Buck Pond, at mile 7.3.

The trail no[w ...]adorned with extremely large red spruce, hemlock and yellow birch. The forest here could be an extension of the old-growth northern hardwood parcel W of the river from near Griffin Rapids to the vicinity of Big Otter Pond.

The trail descends into an extensive wooded ~~~~~ amp, partially the result of beaver flooding along He~~~~~~~~~~~ trail and yellow disks may be obs~~~~~~~~~~~~~~~~~~~~~~~~~nding on beaver activity and tr~~~~

Finally, at 8~~~~~~~~~~~~~~~~~~~~~~~~~ esker with large conifers cr~~~~~~~~~~~~~~~~~~~~ct of Cage Lake is crossed as it ca~~~~~~~~~~~~ beaver dam to a large marshy vlei beneath it. F~~~~~ ~~~ dam a view can be had down the length of the lake. A wooded peninsula (actually another esker) splits the lake into two sections. Loons and brook trout inhabit both. The Cage Lake lean-to is located just beyond this point.

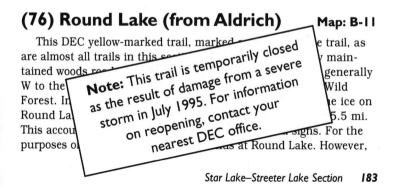

Note: This trail now terminates at Buck Pond, at mile 7.3.

Trail in winter: *Generally suitable for skiing until Buck Pond, then twisting and wetness make it less suitable. Back portions are quite remote and skiers should be adequately prepared.*

Distances: *Youngs Rd. to old Buck Pond trail, 1.1 mi.; to Little Otter Pond, 2.1 mi.; to gate, 5.5 mi.; to Buck Pond, 7.3 mi. (11.7 km).*

(76) Round Lake (from Aldrich)   Map: B-11

This DEC yellow-marked trail, marked ~~~~~~~~~ e trail, as are almost all trails in this ~~~~~~~~~~~~~~~~~~~ y maintained woods ro~~~~~~~~~~~~~~~~~~~~~~~~~~~ generally W to the ~~~~~~~~~~~~~~~~~~~~~~~~~~~~~~~~~~ Wild Forest. In ~~~~~~~~~~~~~~~~~~~~~~~~~~~~~~~~ e ice on Round La~~~~~~~~~~~~~~~~~~~~~~~~~~~~~~~~5.5 mi. This accou~~~~~~~~~~~~~~~~~~~~~~~~~~~~~igns. For the purposes o~~~~~~~~~~~~~~~~~~~~s at Round Lake. However,

Note: This trail is temporarily closed as the result of damage from a severe storm in July 1995. For information on reopening, contact your nearest DEC office.

a bushwhack along the shores of Round Lake for approximately 1.0 mi., joining the terminus of the Kalurah-Round Lake Trail (trail 77), makes a hike of approximately 10.0 mi. one way. This trip can be make from Aldrich to Kalurah in the summer. Kalurah, like Aldrich, is an abandoned lumbering community now composed mainly of scattered hunting camps.

Trailhead: *The trailhead is on the R, 1.5 mi. from Aldrich on the privately maintained woods road to Streeter Lake. Access to Aldrich is detailed in the Streeter Lake Ski Trail (trail 78) description.*

The trial crosses a hardwood forest with occasional red spruce present at the outset. At 0.5 mi. a DEC sign states: "Kalurah 9.0 mi." This should be ignored. The references here are to the snow-mobile trail noted above, which crosses the ice in winter.

The trail passes a beaver pond at 0.6 mi. and then a small creek on a narrow wooden bridge at 0.8 mi. The terrain now begins to undulate steeply with occasional large yellow birch and spruce in sight. The trail crosses two more small creeks on wooden bridges at 1.1 mi. and 1.3 mi. After crossing the second bridge the trail goes sharply L, now following red trail markers. The yellow-marked trail previously followed forks to the R and shortly enters an extensive wet spruce swamp which is not suitable for hiking.

The trail, following the red markers, begins a climb up a steep ridge crowned with large beech and sugar maples. On top there is much evidence of blowdown, fortunately usually off to the side of the trail. At 2.0 mi. the trail crosses Long Lake at its outlet on a wooden bridge. This lake is aptly named, long and narrow with all but its upper portion in the Forest Preserve.

The trail now begins to rise again, starting its climb over another long beech-lined ridge. It begins a gradual descent from this ridge to the shores of Round Lake at 3.4 mi. This large, circular lake, also aptly named, has majestic specimens of white pine on its shore and a solitary island in its middle. Loons can be heard calling from the lake in the summer. At this point the hiker has an option of bushwhacking for approximately 1.0 mi. to the R along the lakeshore and then using the Kalurah-Round Lake Trail to reach Kalurah for a total hike of about 10.0 mi. Otherwise it is a round trip of 6.8 mi. back to the trailhead of the Aldrich-Streeter Lake Road.

Trail in winter: Generally not suitable after 1.0 mi. Steep and twisting.

Distances: Streeter Lake Rd. to Long Lake, 2.4 mi.; to Round Lake, 3.4 mi. (5.4 km).

(77) Round Lake (from Kalurah)   Map: A-11

This DEC red-marked snowmobile trail goes generally E from the vicinity of the abandoned hamlets of Jayville and Kalurah to arrive at the opposite side of Round Lake from the Aldrich-Round Lake Trail (trail 76). Kalurah and Jayville were f̶o̶r̶ ̶ ̶ ̶ ̶ ̶ ̶ ̶ ̶g hamlets based on the lumbering and m̶ ̶ ̶ ̶ ̶ ̶ ̶ ̶ ̶ ̶ vely. When the timber and ir̶ ̶ ̶ ̶ ̶ ̶ ̶ ̶ ̶ ̶ ̶ ̶ ̶ ̶ n of the century, ̶ ̶ ̶ ̶ ̶ ̶ ̶ ̶ ̶ ̶ ̶ ̶ ̶ ̶ ̶ ̶ ̶ rustic hunting ̶ ̶ ̶ ̶ ̶ ̶ ̶ ̶ ̶ ̶ ̶ ̶ ̶ ̶ ̶ ̶ g.

Althou̶ ̶ ̶ ̶ ̶ ̶ ̶ ̶ ̶ ̶ ̶ ̶ ̶ ̶ ̶ ̶ ̶ r DEC, severe bea̶ ̶ ̶ ̶ ̶ ̶ ̶ ̶ ̶ ̶ ̶ ̶ ̶ ̶ ̶mits for all intents and ̶ ̶ ̶ ̶ ̶ ̶ ̶ ̶ ̶ ̶gins on the extension of the Kalurah̶ ̶ ̶ ̶ ̶ ̶ ̶om NY 3 and 0.3 mi. before Forest Preserve lan̶ ̶ ̶ ̶ reached. This spot is approximately 0.4 mi. past the old gravel pit parking area, which has now been posted. Unfortunately, the beaver dam, which has flooded the road for 150 yds. here up to a depth of four feet in places, is not located on the

Note: This trail is temporarily closed as the result of damage from a severe storm in July 1995. For information on reopening, contact your nearest DEC office.

roadway here but 100 yds. upstream. The contour of the land must be followed here to make a rather difficult crossing on the dam. However, the land is strictly posted against trespassing and permission to enter it will probably not be granted. The roadbed itself is owned by DEC directly. Ultimately this condition will be rectified with projected implementation of the unit management plan for the Aldrich Pond Wild Forest, perhaps in 1994, but until then the trail must be deemed unattainable.

The first 100 yds. of the trail when it has reached the Forest Preserve are also flooded. Maintenance has been minimal; many disks are missing and minor beaver flooding occurs also in the upper portion of the trail.

Trailhead: *Access is from the continuation of the Kalurah Road as it becomes a trail using the bed of an old logging railroad upon entering the Forest Preserve. To reach the Kalurah Road proceed E on NY 3, 2.0 mi. from the village of Harrisville. At this point the Kalurah Rd. comes in sharply on the R. This point is also 20.0 mi. W of the village of Star Lake. The Kalurah Road goes S from NY 3, running steadily uphill until it crosses the tracks of the Carthage Central Railroad for the final time. This is at a point approximately 3.5 mi. from NY 3 and is the site of the old hamlet of Kalurah.*

Shortly after crossing the railroad tracks the road forks. The L fork leads to the abandoned mines at Jayville, now mostly on private land. Take the R fork and proceed another 0.8 mi. until a gravel pit on the L just before a metal bridge crossing a creek. This was formerly a parking spot, but is now off limits. Proceed to the beginning of Forest Preserve land in another 0.7 mi. Park here, or before this point, depending on flooding conditions.

The trail starts as a grassy lane passing through maturing hardwoods with a number of large poplar present. At 0.2 mi. there is a large open beaver vlei on the R. This is a good spot for wildlife viewing.

At 1.0 mi the trail comes to a fork. Trail R is a dead-end

snowmobile trail. The trail continues L until South Creek Lake is reached at 1.6 mi. This lake is noted for its excellent bass fishing. The far shores are private. The trail continues on a mostly level grade through pole-sized hardwoods until the Scuttle Hole is reached on the R at 2.3 mi. The Scuttle Hole is an extremely narrow, marshy lake which probably had its origin in a string of beaver ponds at some time in the past.

The old logging railroad bed is now left behind as the trail makes a turn and proceeds to an old open spirea-studded glade at 3.8 mi. A sign in the middle of the glade points the way to the R where the trail now crosses several open beaver flows before re-entering the forest at 3.4 mi.

A steep ridge with large sugar maple and beech is now ascended and crossed for the next mile until a rather sharp descent is made to the shores of Round Lake at 4.3 mi. The trip back to the trailhead here makes for a round trip of approximately 8.6 mi. For those who wish to bushwhack to the L to reach the end of the Aldrich-Round Lake Trail, a compass reading of 158 degrees across the solitary island in the lake will line up with the end of that trail.

Trail in winter: Not applicable at present due to above condition.

Distances: Forest Preserve boundary to South Creek Lake, 1.6 mi.; to Scuttle Hole, 2.3 mi.; to Round Lake, 4.3 mi. (6.9 km).

(78) Streeter Lake Ski Trail (from Aldrich)

Map: C-11

The trail follows the bed of an old logging railroad which is open to vehicle traffic because of an inholding at Streeter Lake—a small private cemetery—from May through November. It proceeds entirely through the Forest Preserve and links the rustic hamlet of Aldrich and Streeter Lake.

Trailhead: To reach Aldrich, take NY 3 to a blinking traffic signal 2.0 mi. W of Star Lake. Go L at the light and proceed approximately 200 yds. to a T intersection where another L is made. Take this road uphill 0.2 mi. until the Coffin Mills Rd. comes in on the R. It is 3.2 mi. on mostly gravel until a woods road comes in on the L in the hamlet of Aldrich. Park carefully at the side of the road in winter.

A snowmobile base is usually present as the road begins. The trail follows the road bed which with both red and blue disks indicating its dual use as a snowmobile and horse route. The Little River valley floodplain is on the L as the trail goes on a mostly level grade past the Round Lake trailhead on the R at 1.5 mi. Shortly thereafter, Mud Creek is crossed on a wooden bridge at 1.8 mi.

After Mud Creek the trail begins to rise steadily as it crosses several creeks cascading in ravines. These rivulets flow either into Mud Creek or directly into the Little River. An open marsh is crossed at 4.4 mi. just before the trail turns L between the two stone pillars that marked the beginning of the Shuler estate before DEC acquired the land in the 1970s. Ski downhill to a steel gate just beyond Streeter Lake outlet at 4.7 mi.

One may return to Aldrich for a round trip of 9.4 mi. or ski around the gate and cross the potato patch to join the Streeter Lake Trail from Youngs Rd. in the village of Star Lake. If a car is parked on Youngs Rd., this makes for a through ski trip of 8.5 mi.

Trail in Winter: This trail's primary use is as a ski route during the winter months.

Distances: Aldrich to Mud Lake, 1.8 mi.; to Streeter Lake, 4.7 mi. (7.5 km).

(79) Middle Branch Oswegatchie Trail (via Totten–Crossfield)

This trail proceeds S from the outlet of Streeter Lake, passing a loop of the middle branch of the Oswegatchie River on its way to the St. Lawrence-Herkimer County line. Near this line lies the famous old Totten-Crossfield boundary marker. This boundary marker, surveyed by the legendary Verplanck Colvin in the last century, determined the boundaries of most of the land in northern New York. Grades are generally flat and the walking easy until the final segment. The jeep road this trail follows is also for a period the boundary between the Five Ponds Wilderness Area and the Aldrich Pond Wild Forest.

Trailhead: *This trail now begins at the gated end of the Streeter Lake Ski trail (see description, trail 78).*

This is basically the same trail as the Totten–Crossfield trail of the first edition with several variations mainly due to state acquisition of the 16,000-acre Watsons East Triangle tract immediately S of the old trail's termination. The trail, marked with both red snowmobile disks and blue horse trail disks, has been extended another 0.4 mi. into Herkimer County to terminate at a second junction with the Middle Branch of the Oswegatchie River.

Of the three old logging roads branching off at the Log Landing, the one leading straight ahead has been marked by DEC as the trail. This changes the trail's position in relation to the Totten-Crossfield Monument marking the county line boundary and the corner of the Totten-Crossfield Purchase of the Revolutionary War era as relocated by Verplanck Colvin in 1878.

Following an old jeep road, the trail goes around the metal barrier and proceeds under a canopy of tall hardwoods until the old Potato

Patch described earlier in this chapter is reached in 0.2 mi. The trail turns sharply R and follows an old rutted track across this open area for 0.3 mi. The old potato ridges, festooned with a thick carpet of moss, are still readily noticeable in this sandy clearing. With a little luck a woodchuck might be seen. They are the only ones for miles around in an otherwise solid panorama of unbroken forest.

At 0.5 mi. the trail joins the old jeep road (which proceeds along the circumference of the Potato Patch and could be followed as a longer alternative to walking the old rutted path through the sandy field). This jeep trail is followed for all but the last mile or so before the county line.

Passing the Streeter Lake lean-to on the R, the trail goes by the foundations of the buildings that once existed on the private estate at 0.6 mi. The setting here is park-like, pastoral rather than wild, with large specimens of exotic Norway spruce common.

The trail comes to a jct. at 0.8 mi. where it turns L. Just before this turn another jeep trail enters on the L. At 1.0 mi. a side trail comes in on the R. This leads in approximately 100 yds. to the shores of Crystal Lake. This small, circular conifer- and heath-lined lake was used for swimming by the owners of the private estate. A dip in the water will show why. There is a feeling of buoyancy, due to the minerals in the water. The same minerals probably account for the clarity of the water and also for the fact that the lake was reputed to be without fish long before the era of acid rain.

The trail continues through pole-sized hemlock and red spruce until another side trail enters L at 1.4 mi. This trail dead-ends in 300 yds. at Tamarack Creek. At 1.7 mi. a beaver dam appears across the trail; crossing can usually be made on the dam itself. This is the outlet of Pansy Pond; DEC is considering abandoning the trail at this point in the pending Unit Management Plan. This would probably not be enacted for several years.

At 2.1 mi. the trail heads R while a trail L goes over Francis Hill and rejoins the main trail after 1.7 mi. At 2.4 mi. the trail reaches a wide loop on the middle branch of the Oswegatchie River on the R. This spot makes a pleasant, informal campsite. The trail continues S as it passes through a classic spruce/fir swamp with occasional glimpses of the river and its balsam-lined corridor on the R. At 3.0 mi. another beaver flow is encountered; crossing is again made on the dam.

At 3.6 mi. the trail bears R at a junction. Trail L is the Francis Hill Trail rejoining the main Totten-Crossfield Trail. At 3.8 mi. Bassett Creek is crossed on a wooden bridge. The beaver here have a tendency to try to dam the area under the bridge and flood the trail. However, local DEC personnel are usually quick to respond and as a result the bridge is usually passable. Bassett Creek is another one of those streams, not uncommon in this area, that flow through Forest Preserve lands for their entire length.

At 4.1 mi. the jeep trail disappears at an old, roughly circular log landing. Timber was previously taken to this spot for hauling out of the area via the jeep road. Follow the markers on the trail straight ahead as it passes through a mostly hardwood forest that was subject to heavy logging before state acquisition in the 1970s.

At 5.0 mi. the trail enters a spruce swamp and continues through it for a short distance. At 5.1 mi. the trail passes the remnants of old logging and hunting camps with a stone fireplace still standing. Several outbuildings remain in a collapsed state – the granite Totten-Crossfield marker set in place in 1903 over the spot where Verplank Colvin placed his monument now lies hidden in the forest close to 200 yds. from the trail. It is reached by taking a compass reading of 135° from the last demolished outbuilding. The going is rough, as conifer growth is thick here, so caution has to be exercised if an attempt is made to locate the monument.

At 5.2 mi. the county line is passed and the trail passes on to the Watsons East Triangle tract recently acquired by DEC. The forest here has not been logged as heavily before state acquisition and this condition is reflected in the large beech and maple encountered on the way.

At 5.6 mi. the trail ends as it meets the Middle Branch of the Oswegatchie River for a second time. Balsam and spruce line the river here. Across its waters lies an interconnecting maze of log roads that eventually lead to the end of Forest Preserve in Lewis County.

Trail in winter: *This trail makes an excellent round trip ski jaunt in winter. Begin after Streeter Lake Ski Trail (trail 78) and keep in mind the remoteness of the setting and the distance if the entire approximately 20.0 mi. trip is contemplated. Be adequately prepared if an attempt is made.*

Distances: *Streeter Lake to Crystal Lake; 1.0 mi.; to Pansy Pond outlet, 1.7 mi.; to first junction with Middle Branch of Oswegatchie, 2.4 mi.; to St. Lawrence-Herkimer County line, 5.2 mi.; to second crossing Middle Branch Oswegatchie, 5.6 mi. (9.0 km).*

Watsons East Triangle Section

State purchase in 1986 of the 16,288-acre Watsons East Triangle Tract consolidated the Pepperbox Wilderness and Wilderness Lake Primitive Area on the S with the Aldrich Pond Wild Forest on the N and was a pivotal acquisition of a key inholding in the projected Bob Marshall-Oswegatchie Great Forest. The hunting club leases expired in September 1991 and the remaining hunting camps were destroyed or removed at that time.

The main logging road extends 10.8 mi. as a graveled, twisting thoroughfare that ends where a DEC barrier gate bars further vehicular progress. It can be driven with caution to this point but is much better suited to 4WD vehicles. The road inside the gate can be walked another 4.3 mi. to the posted signs of a private inholding.

This main haul road, unplowed in winter but usually with a firm snowmobile base, provides a lengthy cross-country ski trek. It is also ideally suited to a bicycle tour at other times of year. Traffic is scarce, generally only a few vehicles per day. Ancillary log roads which are barred to vehicular traffic lead to a number of the area's abundant ponds.

There is a ranger station in Croghan.

The area is covered by the following USGS topographic maps: Oswegatchie SW 7.5-min. series; Number Four, 7.5 x 15-min. series.

Moderate Hike:

Jakes Pond Trail – *8.6 mi. round trip. This remote hike features a West Branch of the Oswegatchie River crossing and an isolated, attractive glacial pond.*

Trail Described	Total Miles (one way)	Page
Jakes Pond Trail	4.3	194
Watsons East Main Haul Rd. Trail	10.8	197
Wolf Pond Trail	0.6	200
Buck Pond Trail	0.3	201
Hog Pond–Tied Lake Trail	1.0	201
Upper South Pond Trail	1.8	202

(80) Jakes Pond Trail   Page Map

This outlying snowmobile trail marked with DEC red markers starts in a remote area of eastern Lewis County and provides the best access to the Watson's East Triangle Wild Forest. The trail proceeds in a SW direction, following mostly moderate grades to the Forest Preserve parcel. Beaver flooding impedes the way in a few areas, but this is more than offset by the views of the little-known W branch of the Oswegatchie River afforded along the way.

Trailhead: *The start of the trail is from an area of hunting camps known as Bergrens. Access to Bergrens is from NY 812 in the hamlet of Indian River, 6.0 mi. N of the village of Croghan. Coming from the S, turn R off route 812 onto Erie Canal Rd. here. Proceed E 4.0 mi. to the the hamlet of Belfort, which appears just after a L turn onto Old State Rd. Past Belfort, this is Long Pond Rd. Proceed 3.2 mi. from Belfort to a fork. Go L and continue about 8 mi. to a jeep trail R, 0.7 mi. past the last bridge crossing over the W branch of the*

Oswegatchie River. A parking lot 0.1 mi. down the jeep trail is not currently (1993) accessible; instead, proceed about 200 ft. ahead and park off the road just before a gate that marks the start of the Watsons East main haul road, then return on foot to the parking lot. The trail register lies a little beyond the parking lot.

The trail begins on an easement over private land and climbs a large outcrop of pink granitic gneiss to the head of a waterfall at 0.2 mi. Mostly pole-sized aspen and cherry are passed in this initial stretch of the trail, which gives excellent views of the W branch of the Oswegatchie River on the L.

At 1.0 mi. the trail crosses the river on a long wooden bridge with extensive tamarack and spruce-lined wetlands fringing the river on both sides. The wetlands here are reminiscent of the wetlands along the main branch of the Oswegatchie River at High Rock. One difference is the presence of occasional wild azalea in these wetlands. This beautiful pink-blooming shrub is entirely lacking in the more boreal wetlands along the main branch.

At 1.2 mi. the trail crosses a flooded area on a beaver dam. At 1.3 mi. an esker is ascended and red spruce and balsam fir become more prevalent. At 1.6 mi. the trail enters the Forest Preserve and proceeds over exposed bedrock at 1.8 mi., passing through cut-over hardwoods with patches of poverty grass still remaining under them.

At trail jct. at 2.0 mi. the trail goes R. At 2.2 mi. the way is again impeded by beaver flooding. A short bushwhack to the R is necessary to avoid the flooded area. At 2.6 mi. the trail negotiates a handsome stand of tamarack. Shortly thereafter hardwoods predominate again. These hardwoods are providing nursery cover for the future forests of the area, young red spruce growing in profusion beneath them.

At 3.4 mi. passage is again impeded by beaver flooding. Once

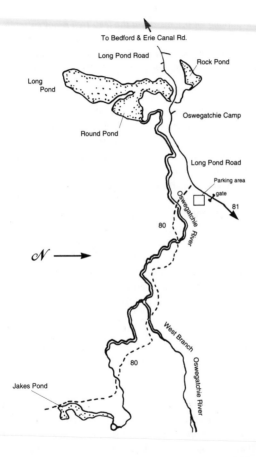

To Bedford & Erie Canal Rd.

Long Pond Road

Rock Pond

Long Pond

Oswegatchie Camp

Round Pond

Long Pond Road

Parking area

gate

81

Oswegatchie River

80

𝒩 ⟶

West Branch Oswegatchie River

80

Jakes Pond

Jakes Pond Trail
Based on Stillwater quadrangle

again a short bushwhack must be made to the R. The trail then ascends another esker and at 4.1 mi. Jakes Pond, visible below, is entirely rimmed by eskers. Its banks are lined with mature hardwoods and occasional conifers. The trail proceeds around Jakes Pond and ends at 4.3 mi at the end of Forest Preserve land. The trail ahead is barred by a gate in a short distance. It is currently on private land and goes S almost to the N boundary of the Pepperbox Wilderness Area.

Trail in winter: Generally not advisable for skiing due to wetlands and bridge crossings. Can be done with caution.

Distances: Bergrens to Oswegatchie bridge, 1.0 mi.; to jct., 2.0 mi., to Jakes Pond, 4.1 mi.; to end of Forest Preserve lands, 4.3 mi. (6.9 km).

(81) Watsons East Main Haul Rd. Trail

Page Map

This is the main access for the area and the route of both a round-trip ski and bicycle tour.

Trailhead: The start of the trail is from an area of hunting camps known as Bergrens. Access to Bergrens is from NY 812 in the hamlet of Indian River, 6.0 mi. N of the village of Croghan. Coming from the S, turn R off route 812 onto Erie Canal Rd. here. Proceed E 4.0 mi. to the the hamlet of Belfort, which appears just after a L turn onto Old State Rd. Past Belfort, this is Long Pond Rd. Proceed 3.2 mi. from Belfort to a fork. Go L and continue about 8 mi. to a jeep trail R, 0.7 mi. past the last bridge crossing over the W branch of the Oswegatchie River. A parking lot 0.1 mi. down the jeep trail is not currently (1993) accessible; instead, proceed about 200 ft. ahead and park off the road just before a gate, then return on foot to the parking lot to sign the trail register

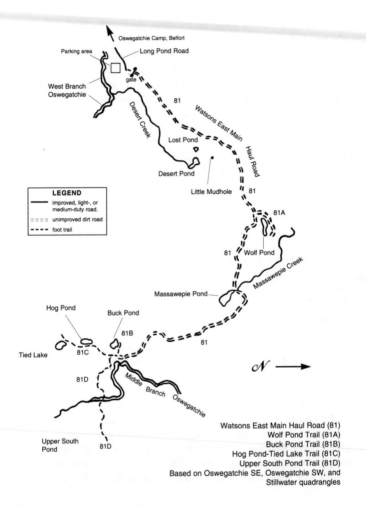

Oswegatchie Camp, Belfort

Parking area — Long Pond Road

West Branch Oswegatchie

gate

Desert Creek

81

Watsons East Main

Lost Pond

Desert Pond

Little Mudhole

Haul Road

81

81A

81

Wolf Pond

Massawepie Creek

Massawepie Pond

Hog Pond   Buck Pond

81B

81C

Tied Lake

81D

Middle Branch Oswegatchie

Upper South Pond

81D

LEGEND
— improved, light-, or medium-duty road.
==== unimproved dirt road
- - - - foot trail

𝒩 ⟶

Watsons East Main Haul Road (81)
Wolf Pond Trail (81A)
Buck Pond Trail (81B)
Hog Pond-Tied Lake Trail (81C)
Upper South Pond Trail (81D)
Based on Oswegatchie SE, Oswegatchie SW, and
Stillwater quadrangles

found just beyond. The gate marks the start of the Watsons East main haul road.

The haul road almost immediately begins a slow ascent of a rather steep hill. The road is quite rocky and winding. At 0.8 mi. the boundary of the Diamond Lassiter Conservation Easement lands is reached; until this point the road is a public right of way through private lands.

Still rising, the road reaches the boundary for Forest Preserve lands at 1.6 mi. The land was lumbered fairly intensively before being acquired by New York State, and as a result a second growth forest of red maple and some white ash is common. These species have glorious fall foliage coloring of blazing red contrasted with amber-purple which usually appears early in September. This is an added incentive to a trip at this time.

A road fork to the left at 4.7 mi. leads to Wolf Pond, described below. Beyond this juncture, the road begins to ascend another steep hill slowly. At 5.8 mi. it reaches the top of the hill and starts a slow descent. The road now becomes generally undulating and winding with several rough areas.

At 6.4 mi. the trail crosses the outlet of Massawepie Pond; a grassy path just before this goes to the pond in 100 yds. The pond is quite marshy but a good place to see ducks.

The road starts to ascend again and, at 9.8 mi., arrives at a locale L known as High Landing. Below this point, at the bottom of a steep cliff, the middle branch of the Oswegatchie River is viewed for the first time, winding its way toward civilization.

At 10.5 mi., another spur road is seen R. This leads to Buck Pond (see below) after a short hike (trail 81B). At 10.6 mi. the road leading to Hog Pond and Tied Lake forks R (trail 81C).

At 10.8 mi. the gate barring further vehicular traffic is reached. A rough parking area is on the L here for those who have had the temerity to drive this far. The road beyond the gate leads in 0.8 mi. to a stand of old growth forest that formerly was a landlocked parcel of state land. It is 4.3 mi. to the boundary line of several private inholdings from that point; this distance may be further skied, walked, or bicycled.

Trail in winter: This trail's primary use, aside from access, could very well be as a round-trip cross-country ski trip (possibly combined with backpacking) and as a bicycle path. The way is wide and winding with several steep hills encountered along the route. Snowmobile traffic, except on weekends, is generally light.

Distances: Start of trail to Forest Preserve, 1.6 mi.; to Wolf Pond fork, 4.7 mi.; to Massawepie Pond outlet, 6.4 mi.; to view of river, 9.8 mi.; to locked gate, 10.8 mi. (17.3 km).

(81A) Wolf Pond Trail

Page Map

Trailhead: Access is from the main haul road (trail 81) at 4.7 mi.

A log road L leads to the pond in 0.2 mi. The pond is rather long and narrow with a mixed forest on its shore, including dead conifers resulting from beaver flooding. Several knolls on the shore make good camping sites, especially where one hunting camp stood. The road continues another 3.0 mi. or so to the Middle Branch of the Oswegatchie, after turns at a number of the ancillary logging roads that cross its path. Beaver flooding is severe in several places and one of the old bridges is out. The conditions regarding beaver flooding can change from year to year depending on the presence of the animals. This route is best undertaken via the assistance of map and compass, particularly after Wolf Pond outlet at 0.6 mi.

Trail in winter: *Trail is suitable for cross-country skiing up to the point where flooding may be encountered.*

Distance: *Main haul road to Wolf Pond, 0.2 mi.; to Wolf Pond Outlet, 0.6 mi. (1.0 km).*

(81B) Buck Pond Trail   Page Map

Trailhead: *Access is from the main haul road (trail 81) at a point where a log road comes in on the R at 10.5 mi.*

This side road leads in 0.3 mi. to Buck Pond, considered the source of the West Branch of the Oswegatchie. A very attractive private camp stood on the pond's shore until 1991.

Trail in winter: *The Buck Pond Trail is suitable for cross-country skiing.*

Distance: *Main Haul Rd. to Buck Road, 0.3 mi. (0.5 km).*

(81C) Hog Pond–Tied Lake Trail   Page Map

Trailhead: *This relatively short trail to two of the area's many modest-sized ponds begins where a log road comes in on the R to intersect the Watsons main haul road (trail 81) at 10.6 mi.*

Public access ends at a gate just past the second pond. The road continues to a private inholding.

The trail starts a slow rise to top an esker at 0.5 mi. where linear-shaped Hog Pond is seen below R. The somewhat marshy shores of the pond are surrounded by a typical mixed Adirondack forest of conifers and hardwoods.

The trail continues to Tied Lake, L at 1.0 mi. Tied Lake, more circular in shape with waters of a dark brown hue from tannic acids, was until 1991 the site of one of the area's many hunting camps. Its outlet, Alder Brook, flows generally SW to the Beaver River.

Trail in winter: *This trail is admirably adapted to cross-country skiing with generally moderate grades. At 1.2 mi. the gate barring further access is encountered.*

Distances: *Main haul road to Hog Pond, 0.5 mi; to Tied Lake, 1.0 mi.; to gate, 1.2 mi. (1.9 km).*

(81D) Upper South Pond Trail   Page Map

Trailhead: *The beginning of the unmarked trail is at the gate at mile 10.8 of the Watsons main haul road (trail 81) which effectively bars further vehicle penetration.*

The trail follows the log road beyond the gate. The path dates back to the turn of the century when it was built as the primary logging road in the region.

At 0.6 mi. the trail turns L to take an ancillary log road to a crossing of the Middle Branch of the Oswegatchie River at 1.0 mi. As this area is now Forest Preserve it is unclear how long the bridge will remain functional. Caution should be exercised here.

At 1.4 mi. at a fork the trail to Upper South Pond goes L. The trail now slowly descends to reach the shores of Upper South Pond at 1.8 mi. An occasional large hemlock and an abundance of marshy shoreline prevail at this point.

Further upstream on the inlet of Upper South Pond lie Middle South and Lower South Pond, both reached only by bushwhacking.

From the turn-off to Upper South Pond Trail, the main haul road leads in a short 0.2 mi. to a parcel of original Forest Preserve that has remained essentially in old growth. The tract, consisting of majestic yellow birch and red spruce, was severely affected by blow-downs in the severe storm of 1950.

Trail in winter: *This trail is generally suitable for cross-country skiing if the bridge over the Middle Branch of the Oswegatchie River is passable.*

Distances: *Gate on main haul road to L turn, 0.6 mi.; to river, 1.0 mi.; to Upper South Pond, 1.8 mi. (2.9 km).*

Stillwater Section

Remote and wild Stillwater Reservoir, resulting from the construction of power dams across the Beaver River, is almost entirely bordered by lands of the Forest Preserve. The 6,700-acre reservoir has not been as seriously affected by acid rain as some of the interior ponds and still supports a sizeable fish population. This is attested to not only by the presence of fishermen but also by the presence of approximately seventeen breeding pairs of loons in 1993 (highest in the Adirondacks) plus the frequent occurrence on the reservoir of that even more dedicated fish eater, the cormorant. There are numerous attractive designated primitive campsites along the shores of the reservoir.

The few trails in this region that are in this guide lead to secluded lakes and ponds, some of them large, all of them quite wild. In addition to a restaurant, there is a DEC Ranger station at the foot of the Reservoir. The unique settlement of Beaver River, reached only by boat or snowmobile in winter, lies approximately 6.0 mi. over the waters and also has a restaurant.

The reservoir is best covered by the recent 7½ x 15 min. Stillwater topographic map.

(82) Red Horse Trail

Page Map

This blue-marked DEC trail leaves the N shore of Stillwater Reservoir and passes several impressive medium-sized glacial lakes on its way to Clear Lake. It is the only trail that gives access to the S portion of the Five Ponds Wilderness Area.

Trailhead: *The trailhead is reached only by a 5.5-mi. boat trip up Stillwater Reservoir from the DEC launch site at the hamlet of Stillwater 27.0 mi. E of the Lewis County village of Lowville on the Stillwater–No. 4 Road.*

The trail begins at Trout Pond on the N shore of Stillwater Reservoir. If the water level of the reservoir is low, the starting point is at Burnt Lake, approximately 0.3 mi. before Trout Pond. Trout Pond and Burnt Lake, both formerly interior lakes, are now flooded bays of Stillwater Reservoir due to the erection of the dam at Stillwater. A lean-to is located just N of the head of Trout Pond.

From Trout Pond the trail proceeds along the bank of Red Horse Creek to Salmon Lake at 1.1 mi. The magnificent stand of climax spruce, hemlock and yellow birch is dwarfed by the occasional gigantic white pine on the shores of the creek.

The trail now skirts the shore of Salmon Lake, passing a lean-to at its head. The trail leaves the lake and passes through a continuous stand of impressive climax forest until a crossing on a plank is made at an extensive beaver-created wetland at 1.9 mi. The trail gradually begins to ascend a modified esker with large spruce and hemlocks again present. It descends from the low ridge to cross several parallel wetlands before reaching Witchhopple Lake at 3.3 mi. The wooden planks used to cross these wetlands can be quite slippery after a rain, so caution should be used.

The trail leaves Witchhopple Lake and proceeds through the same impressive climax forest as before until finally reaching its

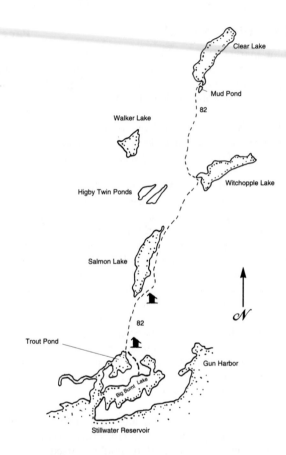

Red Horse Trail (82)
Based on Beaver River quadrangle

206 *Stillwater Section*

ultimate destination on the shores of Clear Lake at 5.3 mi. Wet
spots are encountered in several areas just before the pond.
Summit Mt. looms up protectively over the pond.

Trail in Winter: *Hazardous skiing along Stillwater Reservoir to the trailhead.
Remoteness and occasional rough topography limit skiing from the trailhead.*

Distance: *North shore of Stillwater Reservoir to Salmon Lake, 1.1 mi.; to
Witchhopple Lake, 3.3 mi.; to Clear Lake, 5.3 mi. (8.5 km).*

(83) Raven Lake Jeep Trail   Page Map

This jeep trail was constructed to facilitate logging activities
on the Wilderness Lakes Forest Preserve tract. This tract was
acquired by New York State with a provision providing for the
previous owners to lumber the tract for a period of eight years. The
grace period expired in 1990 and the road, now gated, primarily
provides access for the owners of a small private inholding at
Raven Lake. It also allows hiker penetration of an otherwise
trailless, remote area of the Forest Preserve.

Trailhead: *Access is from Stillwater Reservoir, on the Stillwater-No. 4 Rd.
27.0 mi. E of Lowville. Just before the reservoir, turn L at the Stillwater
Restaurant and take the gravel road 1.2 mi to a DEC parking area on the R
just before a gated wooden bridge spanning the Beaver River, just after the dam
itself is seen to the R. A trail register is located here. The unmarked jeep trail
begins over the bridge.*

The jeep trail begins a series of rolling ascents over wooded
hardwood ridges. After a large gravel pit opening at the outset, the
forest is mostly an intermediate one in the process of maturing. For
part of the way, the jeep trail forms the boundary between the

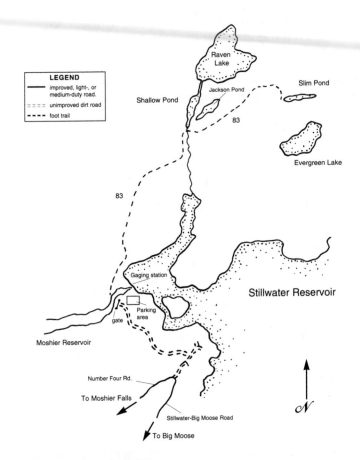

LEGEND

improved, light-, or
medium-duty road.

==== unimproved dirt road

---- foot trail

Raven Lake

Slim Pond

Jackson Pond

Shallow Pond

83

Evergreen Lake

83

Gaging station

Stillwater Reservoir

Parking
area

gate

Moshier Reservoir

Number Four Rd.

To Moshier Falls

Stillwater-Big Moose Road

To Big Moose

N

Raven Lake Jeep Trail (83)
Based on Stillwater quadrangle

Wilderness Lakes tract and the Pepperbox Wilderness.

As the trail continues over several hills, the forest displays the recent logging on the Wilderness Lake tract. One bonus from this heavy cutting is the profusion of blackberry and red raspberry bushes along the road.

At 2.1 mi. Shallow Pond is seen on the L. It is connected by a short channel to Raven Lake, a handsome 70-acre body of water surrounded by hills on one side. Evergreens are common along the two shorelines, in contrast to the ridges, which are generally comprised of hardwoods.

This is the highlight of the jeep trail, but it does go approximately another mile until ending at a large log landing. Before that another jeep road goes R at approximately 2.5 mi. to arrive at Slim Pond at 3.4 mi. Slim Pond is another long, shallow body of water nestled between wooded ridges. The path of the jeep trail is blocked by boulders just after Shallow Pond, as the right of way of the private inholding terminates here, so the condition of the trail from Shallow Pond to Slim Pond can be expected to deteriorate barring any unforeseen circumstance.

Trail in winter: *The entire jeep trail to Slim Pond makes for an excellent round-trip ski jaunt in winter. Exercise caution going over the bridge at the outset!*

Distances: *Trailhead to Shallow Pond 2.1 mi.; to Slim Pond: 3.4 mi. (5.4 km).*

(84) Pepperbox Wilderness Access Trail
Page Map

This short bridge-crossing trail, currently provides the only marked access to the unique Pepperbox Wilderness Area. This isolated wilderness, which is the SW tier of the unbroken forest

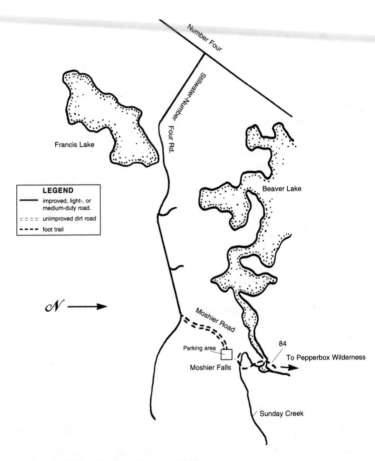

Pepperbox Wilderness Access Trail (84)
Number Four quadrangle

stretching from the Oswegatchie to the Beaver River drainage, is entirely trailless and possesses some of the most unaltered wetland ecosystems in the entire Adirondack Park. The trail is marked with Niagara Mohawk blazes and with the DEC blue disks.

Trailhead: *Access is off the Stillwater-No. 4 Road, a gravel road going from the village of Lowville in Lewis County to the Stillwater Reservoir. From Lowville it is 18.0 mi. on the No. 4 Road to the junction of the Stillwater Road. Bear R on the Stillwater Road and proceed another 2.1 mi. until Moshier Road comes in L. This is at a spot approximately 7.0 mi. from Stillwater Reservoir. Proceed 0.6 mi. on the Moshier Road until a DEC parking lot is seen on the R.*

The trail to the Pepperbox Wilderness begins across the road from the parking lot. From the trail register at the parking lot, another red-marked trail proceeds 0.3 mi. to give access to the Independence Wild Forest.

The trail we take goes 0.4 mi. over Niagara Mohawk land to the Pepperbox Wilderness, where it ends. At 0.1 mi., it crosses Sunday Creek on a bridge. The trail veers R to cross the wide Beaver River on a much longer wooden bridge at 0.2 mi. The trail then crosses a heavily cut-over area with a dense undergrowth of brambles before arriving at the Forest Preserve boundary at 0.4 mi.

Trail in winter: *Limited by brevity of trail.*

Distances: *Moshier Rd. to Beaver River, 0.2 mi.; to Forest Preserve boundary, 0.4 mi. (0.6 km).*

Appendix I

Glossary of Terms

Bushwhacking   To make one's way through bushes or undergrowth without the aid of a formal trail.

Corduroy   A road, trail or bridge formed by logs laid side by side transversely to facilitate crossing swampy areas.

Esker   A long, winding ridge created by water running under or upon an Ice Age glacier. Prevalent in northern region. Soils layered and quite dry. Tops of ridge usually crowned with conifers.

Jeep trail   A woods road that is still occasionally used by 4WD and all-terrain vehicles.

Kettle   A depression in the ground created by late-melting ice during glacial times. Usually occupied in this region by a pond or lake, or their aftermath, a northern bog.

Lean-to   A three-sided shelter with an over-hanging roof on the open side.

Tote road   An old logging road that is now generally confined to foot travel.

Vlei   A marshy open area, usually the aftermath of a beaver pond filling in (pronounced "vly").

Appendix II

Table of Short Hikes

For the benefit of those looking for easy introductions to the Northern Region, the following table lists destinations of less than 2.5 mi. (one way) from shortest to longer for each section in this guide. This table should help hikers unfamiliar with the region to identify worthwhile intermediate destinations within longer hikes. Each significant destination is listed separately with, in some cases, multiple destinations on one trail. The name and number of the complete trail description are included. In this region of generally moderate relief, walking time will, in most instances, conform to the actual distances traversed with the exception of the relatively modest climb to the Bear Mt. lean-to, which may take somewhat longer.

Many of these hikes are ideal for children. See the section on "Hiking with Children" in the Introduction of this guide.

Dist.	Objective	Trail Name & Number
LONG LAKE SECTION		
1.3 mi.	Grassy Pond	Sargent Pond Loop (1)
TUPPER LAKE SECTION		
0.9 mi.	Follensby Clear Pond	Floodwood Loop (13)
0.5 mi.	Copperas Pond	Otter Hollow Loop (14)

Dist.	Objective	Trail Name & Number
0.9 mi.	Whey Pond	Otter Hollow Loop (14)
2.2 mi.	Little Square Pond	Otter Hollow Loop (14)

PAUL SMITHS SECTION

0.7 mi.	Church Pond Lean-to	Red Dot Loop (23)

DeBAR WILD FOREST

0.5 mi.	Osgood River	Hayes Brook Truck Trail (26)

CLEAR POND WILD FOREST

0.6 mi.	Little Rock Pond	Lilypad Pond Trail (39)

STAR LAKE

0.8 mi.	Little River	Streeter Lake (Amo Rd.) (73)
0.3 mi.	Tamarack Creek	Streeter Lake (Youngs Rd.) (74)
2.1 mi.	Little Otter Pond	Cage Lake (via Boundary Trail) (75)
1.0 mi.	Crystal Lake	Middle Br. Oswegatchie (79)
2.4 mi.	Long Lake	Round Lake (Aldrich) (76)
1.6 mi.	South Creek Lake	Round Lake (Kalurah) (77)

WATSONS EAST TRIANGLE

1.0 mi.	W. Branch Oswegatchie River	Jakes Pond Trail (80)

STILLWATER SECTION

1.1 mi.	Salmon Lake	Red Horse Trail (82)
2.1 mi.	Shallow Pond	Raven Lake Jeep Trail (83)

CRANBERRY LAKE SECTION

0.8 mi.	DEC Lean-to	Bear Mt. Trail (55)

Appendix III

Opportunities in the Region for Some People with Disabilities

The following is a list of access opportunities in the Northern region for people who use wheelchairs or have other physical limitations. **These trails and access points do not conform to formal accessibility standards and are subject to changes in weather conditions.**

The trails in this rugged region of the Adirondacks are challenging for all visitors. Before undertaking trail or boat trips, users of the appendix may find it helpful to have a friend knowledgeable about their capabilities scout the trip beforehand.

Scenic Vistas

The heavily wooded aspect of this region eliminates most panoramic views and the relatively moderate terrain makes for few awe-inspiring peaks in the distance. Still, pleasing vistas can occasionally be found along the region's highways.

Dead Creek parking area. S side of NY 3 approximately 8.0 mi. W of Tupper Lake. An unimproved parking area provides a superb view of Mt. Matumbla, St. Lawrence County's highest point, N down Dead Creek toward its confluence with the Raquette River. Recent (December 1992) acquisition by the state of land in this area may mean the appearance of a trail sometime soon.

Grass River parking area. S side of NY 3 approximately 3.0 mi. E of a pleasant conifer forest adjacent to Forest Preserve land and the Grass River. A large deer wintering yard in the vicinity attracts bald eagles to feed on deer killed by coyotes and vehicles.

Tooley Pond Road. This road runs W from a point on NY 3 just W of the Oswegatchie River bridge in Cranberry Lake, 18.0 mi. to the hamlet of DeGrasse. The W 14.0 mi. proceed through paper company lands, with only an occasional rustic hunting camp to be seen. The South Branch of the Grass River parallels the road for several miles, with tantalizing views of several large waterfalls perceivable on the heavily posted properties. The main attraction of the road is the abundant wildlife likely to be spotted, including deer, fox, coyote and bear.

NY 86. Traveling E from Paul Smiths, one can find superb landscapes of farmland—rare in the Adirondack Park—backed by Whiteface Mt. and other High Peaks.

NY 374 from Lyon Mt. to Dannemora. This well-maintained road descends a shoulder of Lyon Mt., the descent from which provides marvelous panoramas of the High Peaks, the Lake Champlain valley and Vermont.

Trail Access

Streeter Lake Ski Trail (trail 78). This 4.7 mi. narrow gravel road through Forest Preserve lands receives light vehicle pressure during spring and summer. It is heavily used by hunters in autumn. Grades are level to moderate with only one relatively steep pitch.

High Falls Loop (trail 58). The first 1.8 mi. of this long loop, to the jct. with the Leary Trail, is almost completely level. This is a former truck trail, now a grassy path. Most of this section is classified as a Primitive Corridor; with the exception of an occasional vehicle from the Wanakena Water Company, it is not driven.

Slush Pond Ski Trail (trail 28). During non-winter months this is a lightly traveled gravel town road that proceeds 2.5 mi. through Forest Preserve lands to provide access to a large private estate. The gravel is hard-packed and the grade is moderate the entire distance.

Boat Access

There are several boat launching sites adjacent to roads in the region where a boat may be put in for a trip away from a road into the Forest Preserve and surrounding wild lands.

Long Lake. An official DEC boat launching site is in the hamlet of Long Lake, 22.0 mi. south of Tupper Lake on NY 30.

Lake Eaton Campground. Approximately 1.0 mi. N of Long Lake on NY 30. Boats may be launched on Lake Eaton from the park road.

Tupper Lake. An official DEC boat launching site is located just outside the village of Tupper Lake, on the W side of NY 30 0.2 mi S of the Raquette River bridge.

Fish Creek Campground. Boats can be launched at this campground, 10.0 mi. N of Tupper Lake on NY 30. Fish Creek Pond is adjacent to the park road; from it, one can boat into other ponds and Upper Saranac Lake.

Meacham Lake. A DEC parking area on the E side of NY 30 just N of its junction with NY 458 gives access to the outlet of Meacham Lake and, along the lake's S shore, the Osgood River.

Cranberry Lake. A DEC boat launching site is located E of

Columbian Rd., 0.2 mi. S of NY 3 in the hamlet of Cranberry Lake.

Streeter Lake. Boats may be launched onto the outlet of Streeter Lake where a gate marks the end of the DEC-maintained Streeter Lake Rd.

Stillwater. Boats may be launched from a large DEC boat launching facility onto Stillwater Reservoir. The site is located at the end of Stillwater Rd., 27.0 mi. E of Lowville, adjacent to the DEC Stillwater Ranger Station.

The Department of Environmental Conservation (DEC) produces a brochure, "Opening the Outdoors to People with Disabilities," available from the DEC, 50 Wolf Rd., Albany, NY 12233.

DEC also provides a free permit for physically impaired people who want to take a motor vehicle onto a normally restricted access road in Wild Forest areas. Allow three to four weeks' lead time for obtaining this permit. There is no restriction on the use of motorized wheelchairs (as long as they are the kind used in the home) in Wilderness areas. Consult DEC at the above address for further information.

Appendix IV

Lean-tos in the Northern Region

The following is a listing of all lean-tos within the area covered by this guidebook. They are listed by book section, with USGS map and general location; sections not listed have no lean-tos..

Shelter	USGS Map	Location
LONG LAKE SECTION		
Tioga Pt. (several)	Raquette Lake	at end of Tioga Pt. Tr. – 3.2 mi. from trailhead
Lake Lila	Raquette Lake	at 2.8 mi. of Lake Lila – Frederica Mt. Tr.
TUPPER LAKE SECTION		
Fish Pond 1	St. Regis 7½ x 15'	end of Fish Pond Tr. – 5.1 mi. from trailhead, along shore
Fish Pond 2	St. Regis 7½ x 15'	on far shore, reachable only by canoe
DeBAR WILD FOREST		
DeBar Mt.	DeBar Mt.	1.8 mi. along DeBar Mt. Tr.
Sheep Meadow 1 & 2	Meacham Lake	end of Hayes Brook Truck Tr. – 3.6 mi. from trailhead

Shelter	USGS Map	Location

CRANBERRY LAKE–WANAKENA SECTION

Shelter	USGS Map	Location
Burntbridge Pond	Piercefield 7½ x 15'	end of Burntbridge Pond Tr. – 6 mi.
Bear Mt.	Cranberry Lake	0.8 mi. along Bear Mt. Tr. (from NY 3)
High Falls 1 & 2	Five Ponds	6.2 mi. along High Falls Loop
Big Shallow	Five Ponds	2.8 mi. along Sand Lake Trail
Little Shallow	Five Ponds	3.4 mi. along Sand Lake Trail
Sand Lake	Oswegatchie SE	end of Sand Lake Trail at 7.2 mi.
Wolf Pond	Five Ponds	0.5 mi. along Cage Lake Tr. (from Sand Lake)
Griffin Rapids	Five Ponds	on Oswegatchie River, reachable only by canoe
Cage Lake Springhole	Five Ponds	on Oswegatchie River, reachable only by canoe
Cowhorn Pond	Wolf Mt.	0.2 mi. along Cowhorn Pond Trail
Olmstead Pond	Wolf Mt.	1.2 mi. along Olmstead Pond Loop
Janacks Landing	Five Ponds	0.2 mi. end of Janacks Landing trail

STAR LAKE SECTION

Shelter	USGS Map	Location
Streeter Lake	Oswegatchie SE	0.5 mi. along Middle Br. Oswegatchie Trail

Shelter	USGS Map	Location
Cage Lake	Oswegatchie SE	End of Cage Lake Boundary Tr. – 8.4 mi. from trailhead

STILLWATER SECTION

Trout Pond	Big Moose	start of Red Horse Trail – N of Lake
Salmon Lake	Big Moose	1.1 mi. long Red Horse Trail

Appendix V

State Campgrounds in the Northern Region

Public campgrounds have been established by the DEC at many attractive spots throughout the state. Listed below are those campgrounds which might be useful as bases of operations for hiking in the Northern Region. A complete listing of all campgrounds is contained in a brochure of New York State Forest Preserve Public Campgrounds titled "Come Back Next Summer." This brochure is available from the DEC, 50 Wolf Rd., Albany, NY 12233.

Below are the campgrounds in the Northern Region. The first five are on or within a short distance of NY 30, and are listed from S to N; the sixth is in the western part of the region.

Forked Lake. 3.0 mi. S of Long Lake on NY 30, take Deerland Road 2.8 mi. to fork, turn right to end of road.

Lake Eaton. On NY 30, 2.0 mi. N of Long Lake.

Fish Creek/Rollins Pond. On NY 30, 12.0 mi. N of Tupper Lake. Large campgrounds with good boating and swimming.

Buck Pond. On Rainbow Lake near Onchiota, between NY 30 and NY 3.

Meacham Lake. On NY 30, 19.0 mi. N or Lake Clear Jct. Spacious campground with excellent beach.

Cranberry Lake. From Cranberry Lake village, 1.0 mi. S of NY 3 on Campsite Rd.

Index

Note: Lakes are listed under their names instead of under "Lake."

Dawn on St. Regis Pond

Betsy Tisdale

Everton Falls Trail

Everton Falls is a 530-acre nature preserve that straddles the East Branch of the St. Regis River on the N edge of the Adirondack Park. Acquired by the Adirondack Nature Conservancy in 1974 and maintained by volunteers, it takes its name from a thriving 19th-century logging hamlet. The conservancy has constructed a short, easy self-guiding nature trail, The Hardwoods Trail, through the tract. The tract also offers canoe access to a 10-mile stillwater above the falls, an 18-foot series of plunges over rock ledges.

Trailhead: The Hardwoods Trail begins on the Red Tavern Rd (Franklin County Rt. 14), approximately 8.0 mi. W of the intersection of NY 30 and NY 99 at Duane Corners. (The Red Tavern Rd. is an extension of NY 99.) The trailhead is approximately 7.0 mi. E of St. Regis Falls. Look for a small parking area with a recessed post on the N side of the road, about 100 yds. E of a private camp. Interpretive brochures are available here, or from the conservancy at 518-576-2082.

The trail heads NE into the woods, soon swinging NW as it passes a beaver pond on the R. It passes through mixed hardwood forest that is regenerating after years of intensive logging. Dominant species are black cherry, yellow birch, red and sugar maple, and American beech, with some balsam fir evident, especially in low areas. Lichens, ferns, shrubs and ground-cover plants are clearly identified in the brochure as a demonstration of forest succession.

The trail joins the grade of a long-abandoned logging railroad. It soon leaves the old roadbed and passes through a clearing, one of several that mark the site of Everton, the logging community that was deserted in the 1890s. The trail reaches Everton Rd., at one time a section of the famous Port Kent–Hopkinton Turnpike, at about 0.5 mi. A turn L on this road and another in a short distance onto Red Tavern

Rd. will bring one back to the trailhead at 1.0 mi.

Distances: *Trailhead to Everton Rd., 0.5 mi.; to trailhead, 1.0 mi. (0.6 km).*

NOTES

NOTES

NOTES

Other Publications of
The Adirondack Mountain Club, Inc.
814 Goggins Rd.
Lake George, N.Y. 12845-4117
(518) 668-4447

B O O K S

85 Acres: A Field Guide to the Adirondack Alpine Summits
Forests & Trees of the Adirondack High Peaks Region
Adirondack Canoe Waters: North Flow
Adirondack Canoe Waters: South & West Flow
The Adirondack Mt. Club Canoe Guide to Western & Central New York State
Classic Adirondack Ski Tours
Winterwise: A Backpacker's Guide
Climbing in the Adirondacks
Guide to Adirondack Trails: High Peaks Region
Guide to Adirondack Trails: Central Region
Guide to Adirondack Trails: Northville–Placid Trail
Guide to Adironadack Trails: West-Central Region
Guide to Adirondack Trails: Eastern Region
Guide to Adirondack Trails: Southern Region
Guide to Catskill Trails
An Adirondack Sampler, Day Hikes for All Seasons
An Adirondack Sampler II, Backpacking Trips
Geology of the Adirondack High Peaks Region
The Adirondack Reader
Our Wilderness: How the People of New York Found, Changed, and
Preserved the Adirondacks
Adirondack Wildguide (distributed by ADK)
With Wilderness of Heart:
A Short History of the Adirondack Mountain Club

M A P S

Trails of the Adirondack High Peaks Region
Trails of the Northern Region
Trails of the Central Region
Northville–Placid Trail
Trails of the West-Central Region
Trails of the Eastern Region
Trails of the Southern Region

Price list available on request.

Backdoor to Backcountry

ADKers choose from friendly outings, for those just getting started with local chapters, to Adirondack backpacks and international treks. Learn gradually through chapter outings or attend one of our schools, workshops, or other programs. A sampling includes:

- Alpine Flora
- Ice Climbing
- Rock Climbing
- Basic Canoeing
- Bicycle Touring
- Cross-country Skiing

- Mountain Photography
- Winter Mountaineering
- Birds of the Adirondacks
- Geology of the High Peaks

... and so much more!

For more information about the Adirondacks or about ADK...

ADK's Information Center & Headquarters
814 Goggins Rd., Lake George, NY 12845-4117
(518) 668-4447
Exit 21 off I-87 ("the Northway"), 9N South

1st weekend in May–Columbus Day: Mon.–Sat., 8:30–5
Tues. after Columbus Day–1st weekend in May: Mon.–Fri., 8:30–4:30

For more information about our lodges...

ADK Lodges
Box 867, Lake Placid, NY 12946
(518) 523-3441   9 a.m.–7 p.m.
(For reservations or free info re. lodging and programs)

Join A Chapter

Three-quarters of ADK members belong to the chapter in their area. Those not wishing to join a particular chapter join ADK as members at large.

Local chapter membership brings you an easy way to join in the fun of outings and social activities or the reward of working on trails, conservation, and education projects at the local level. And you can still participate in all regular Club activities and receive all the regular benefits.

Adirondak Loj .... North Elba
Albany
Algonquin .... Plattsburgh
Black River .... Watertown
Cold River .... Long Lake
Finger Lakes .... Ithaca-Elmira
Genesee Valley .... Rochester
Glens Falls
Hurricane Mountain .... Keene
Iroquois .... Utica
Keene Valley
Knickerbocker .... New York City & vicinity
Lake Placid
Laurentian .... Canton-Potsdam
Long Island
Mid-Hudson .... Poughkeepsie
Mohican .... Westchester & Putnam counties, NY/Fairfield Co., CT
New York .... Metropolitan Area*
Niagara Frontier .... Buffalo
North Jersey .... Bergen County
North Woods .... Saranac Lake-Tupper Lake
Onondaga .... Syracuse
Ramapo .... Rockland & Orange counties
Schenectady
Shatagee Woods .... Malone
Susquehanna .... Oneonta

*Special requirements apply

Membership
To Join

Call **1-800-395-8080** (Visa, Mastercard or Discover) or send this form with payment to

Adirondack Mountain Club
814 Goggins Rd.
Lake George, NY 12845-4117.

Check Membership Level:

☐ Life $1,000*
☐ Forest Preserve $250*
☐ Patron $125*
☐ Supporting $75*
☐ Contributing $50*
☐ Family $45*
☐ Adult $40
☐ Senior Family $35*
☐ Senior (65+) $30
☐ Junior (under 18) $25
☐ Student (18+, full time) $25

School _____

*Includes associate/family members

Name _____

Address _____

City _____ State ____ Zip ____

Home Telephone ( ) _____

☐ I want to join as a member-at-large.

☐ I want to join as a _____ Chapter member.

List spouse & children under 18 with birthdates:

Spouse _____

Child _____ Birthdate _____

Child _____ Birthdate _____

Bill my: ☐ VISA   ☐ MASTERCARD   ☐ DISCOVER

|__|__|__|__|__|__|__|__|__|__|__|__|__|__|__|__| Exp. date _____

_____
Signature (required for charge)

ADK is a non-profit, tax-exempt organization. Membership fees are tax deductible, as allowed by law. Please allow 6-8 weeks for receipt of first issue of **Adirondac.**

Prices subject to change.

Adirondack
ADK
Mountain Club

GNR

Membership Rewards

- **Discovery:**
  ADK can broaden your horizons by introducing you to new places, recreational activities, and interests.

- **Enjoyment:**
  Being outdoors more and loving it more.

- **People:**
  Meeting others and sharing the fun.

- *Adirondac* Magazine.

- **Member Discounts:**
  20% off on ADK publications, 10% on ADK lodge stays, and reduced rates for educational programs.

- **Satisfaction:**
  Knowing you're doing your part and that future generations will enjoy the wilderness as you do.

Adirondack **ADK** Mountain Club

Conservation

Recreation

Education